Continuous Improvement Strategy - A Business Leader's Guide to Selecting, Deploying and Sustaining a Successful Continuous Improvement Program

Continuous Improvement Strategy - A Business Leader's Guide to Selecting, Deploying and Sustaining a Successful Continuous Improvement Program

Dave Bhattacharya and JP Gnanam

Hardcover ISBN 978-1-105-69658-9
Paperback ISBN 978-1-105-69659-6

This book is dedicated to my Baba on his 80th Birthday. Also dedicated to Ma, my wife Deblina, and my little diamond, Akshaj – DB

Dedicating this book to my biggest inspiration and supporter in the world, my mother, Rajavalli Gnanam – JPG

Table of Contents

Foreword.. ix

Introduction.. xiii

Chapter 1 – The Need for Continuous Improvement 1

Chapter 2 – How Relevant is Six Sigma and Lean Today 15

Chapter 3 – Choosing the Right Continuous Improvement
              Methodology – Lean or Six Sigma? 25

Chapter 4 – Continuous Improvement in the ITIL, SCOR,
              CMMI, PMBOK and ISO World......................35

Chapter 5 – Build Internal Capability or Engage External
              Consultants?...43

Chapter 6 – Establishing the Continuous Improvement
              Organization and Infrastructure...........................51

Chapter 7 – Change Management and Continuous
              Improvement..57

Chapter 8 – Why Continuous Improvement Programs Fail?...69

Chapter 9 – Measurement and Tracking of Continuous
              Improvement Programs 87

Chapter 10 – Final Thoughts 95

Appendix 1 – Assessing an Organization's Change
              Readiness Before Deploying a Six Sigma
              Program...97

Appendix 2 – Application of Continuous Improvement
              Across the Entire Value Chain 101

Appendix 3 – Other Commonly Adopted Continuous
              Improvement Methodologies............................105

Appendix 4 – Why Continuous Improvement Specialists
              Fail? 111

References..113

Foreword

When writing the forward of this book, the objective was to keep alive the spirit of "Customer Focus", the mantra preached by all Quality or Business Excellence professionals. For us, *you* are our customers and hence I have elaborated on the *need* to read and put to practice the principles mentioned in this book. The background of this *customer need* is set in an evolving era of ever increasing levels of customer delight and drastically different perceptions of the way in which every dollar invested can yield multiple times the benefit via differential customer experience and repeat business…leading to greater market share.

The way our industry started a decade ago was purely on a cost benefit resulting from outsourcing or using cheaper resources. Five years down the line the industry evolved to deliver great SLAs consistently. Today all companies boast of near perfect delivery. Where are we poised to go from here? These days, true transformation is expected from our day to day functions. Customers are looking for ways in which we can add value to what has been working smoothly for almost the last decade. This *wow* factor can only come from Value Creation.

"Value Creation is giving the customer what he wants…..before he thinks of it" – Murtaza Poonawala

Dave Bhattacharya and JP Gnanam, in this book, have elaborated the key steps towards selecting the right program based on your customer needs and evolution stage of your organization very well. This would ensure that the program you select is sustainable in the long run and is completely aligned to your company's maturity stage.

Transformation and value creation are *end products* which will come only from a strategy well begun. This statement elaborates the importance of this book. The real - life examples and scenarios written in a fluent story telling manner set the right tone and context to digest the skills that will lead your Quality / Excellence program to success.

Murtaza Poonawala

Dy. General Manager & Head – Business Excellence & Transformation, Syntel, India

[Murtaza Poonawala is a Certified Lean Six Sigma & Project Management Expert. He has led large scale, global deployments at WNS, Avaya & Syntel.]

Foreword

The most striking top of the mind feature of this book is the easy to read and free flowing style in which it is written. The subject is well researched and by providing multiple practical examples as well as case studies from across the globe and from organizations of diverse industry segments, the reading has become very relevant to many practitioners who will always be able to relate to some or the other scenarios. The authors have also kept the rhythm undisturbed by avoiding getting into too many technical details. The level at which this book is written will address the needs of people in leadership and decision making positions. That is where it appears to be directed to in any case. This is not meant to be a technical handbook for black belts or master black belts, and it serves the audience well by remaining focused at a higher level of strategic thought process.

Another thing that is beautifully done in this book is the introduction of multiple other improvement methods and frameworks that have been and are currently in use at various organizations. The introduction of such methods is also kept at an interesting and tantalizing level without getting into too many details that may result in more confusion rather than clarification.

To me, as a leader as well as a practitioner, this has been a very interesting reading as not only it reinforced the strong belief in Six Sigma and Lean it also gave me deeper insight on what is happening around in other organizations. Some of the case studies are absolutely wonderful and turn the old belief upside down. For example, the Chevron case where contrary to popular belief there has been a bottom up success! It is my personal view that all quality methods and frameworks are like religion. Like all religion they all teach the same fundamentals–customer is the most important stakeholder for any organization, being effective *and* efficient at the same time is important, and continuous improvements must be in the DNA of any organization.

And like religion, any methodology or framework that one adopts must be followed with full dedication and discipline as enshrined in the rituals of that particular religion! Six Sigma or Lean or Lean Six Sigma are no different.

Vineet Sharma

Executive Vice President, Quality & Business Excellence
Max New York Life Insurance Co. Limited

Introduction

In our combined twenty-five plus years of industry experience, most of the companies we have come across have treated Six Sigma, Lean, or Total Productivity Maintenance as a tactical tool rather than taking a strategic approach to understand where continuous improvement fits within their corporation and whether it can be applied to the entire business before going ahead with the deployment. At the same time when we look at the list of the top ten companies in the *Fortune 500* for 2011 we find that almost all of them have a visible continuous improvement program. We also looked at a few other published lists of top companies in different areas, and in almost every list the majority of companies follow a continuous improvement program. If these methodologies are indeed working for the best companies out there, we should have expected more widespread understanding of them across most companies. However, as we said right at the beginning, the application of continuous improvement based on overall business strategy has not been really understood or applied by the other thousands of companies out there globally. We both felt that probably there are a lot of questions in the mind of business leaders around continuous improvement–that was the genesis of this book.

Interestingly there is no dearth of success stories from companies who have implemented continuous improvement programs using Lean, Kaizen, Six Sigma or Lean Six Sigma methodologies. One of the most popular early books on Six Sigma titled, *The Six Sigma Way* by Pande, Neuman, and Cavanagh talks about how companies like GE, Motorola, and other top companies have achieved breakthrough performance improvement by embracing and applying the Six Sigma methodology. Likewise, the Lean book *Lean Transformation –*

How to Change Your Business into a Lean Enterprise by Henderson et al has numerous examples of companies that have achieved breakthrough improvement by adopting and applying the Lean methodology. However, even though both the approaches (as well as other methodologies like Total Quality Management, Business Process Management, Hoshin Kanri or Policy Deployment etc.) have been around for almost three decades now, we still come across business leaders who are not clear on what is the right continuous improvement methodology for their companies and how they should go about implementing it and how it fits with their overall strategy. Some have also questioned whether Six Sigma or Lean manufacturing model that Toyota created is still relevant in today's world. (We concede that this is a fair question given the quality struggles and negative press coverage Toyota has seen in the last couple of years). In addition, many of these companies already have ISO, ITIL, CMMI, SCOR or some other compliance or best-in-class process framework in place which increases the complexity of selecting and implementing the correct continuous improvement program or in building the case on how a continuous improvement program can better supplement these best-in-class frameworks.

In our careers as continuous improvement specialists, we have had the opportunity to drive or be part of multiple continuous improvement deployment initiatives in different industries (including one that failed within a year and half of deployment). These were either Six Sigma (or rather Lean Six Sigma) or stand alone Lean/Kaizen initiatives. We have learned a lot from observing how most of these initiatives succeeded and probably even more by closely observing the one that failed. We have been able to see firsthand what went wrong and caused the one deployment initiative to fail and our hope is that by sharing some of our own experience with the readers we will be able to help them in selecting and implementing a successful and sustainable continuous improvement program in their own organization or area of work.

Continuous Improvement has made significant progress from the days of Total Quality Management, Quality Circles and exclusive focus on ISO 9000 (or 9001) certification. The two most popular continuous improvement methodologies in use today by most of the *Fortune 500* companies in some form are Six Sigma and Lean, or some internal framework that has been developed based on these two methodologies. Six Sigma has been around from the mid 1980s but was really popularized by GE in the early 1990s when Jack Welch, the legendary GE CEO, took personal interest in ensuring that it became a way of life within GE and embedded in the culture. Since then it has kept growing in importance as probably the most used methodology for driving improvement across industries. Likewise, Lean has been a relatively old concept as well and had been around for many years. The LEAN philosophy was first introduced in the international bestseller *Kaizen: The Key to Japan's Competitive Success* by Masaki Imai, who is also known as the Father of Kaizen, published in 1986. Subsequently, *The Machine that Changed the World* by Womack, Jones, and Roos, MIT was published in 1990 and helped firmly establish the term Lean to the world. However, it's only in the last decade or so that Lean adoption has taken off in companies outside pure manufacturing. In fact, the adoption rate has been accelerated by combining the concepts of Six Sigma and Lean into what has evolved into Lean Six Sigma. In their book on Lean IT (note: IT as an industry is one of the relative recent adopters of Lean or Six Sigma), authors Bell and Orzen explain how Lean and Six Sigma work together in the IT industry and other services industries as well. They have talked about companies that have started their journey down the continuous improvement (CI) road with Six Sigma mostly since these companies had the right structure and cultural fit in place already and later expanded to Lean (Starwood Hotels and Resort is a great example of a company that successfully deployed and established a Six Sigma program and built that into their culture before moving to Lean deployment to further augment their continuous improvement tool set. This was mentioned in an article that appeared in the March/April 2011 edition of *iSixSigma Magazine*). At the same time there are other companies that chose to go with the Lean approach first, due to the low initial start up costs and rapid results among other benefits. Nowadays many companies are choosing a combination of the two methodologies that gives them the flexibility to pick the right CI tool for the right project from their toolbox.

This book will try to address questions around (1) why companies need continuous improvement (as we mentioned above even in 2012 there are thousands of company who can benefit from a continuous improvement strategy and program), (2) the relevance of continuous improvement in the future (especially given that Lean and Six Sigma have been around for almost twenty-five years now), (3) whether to build the capability in-house or externally, and (4) how companies can assess their readiness to embrace continuous improvement. However, to set the readers expectation properly we would like to make it clear upfront that this book will not get into the step by step details of how a Six Sigma, Lean, Kaizen, Business Process Management or any other continuous improvement methodology can be applied to selected projects within an organization. Our hope is that the material in this book will help business leaders and continuous improvement practitioners better understand which continuous improvement methodology would fit in within their company and how to implement a sustainable and effective continuous improvement program. As for understanding the hands-on application of Six Sigma or Lean/Kaizen approach to projects we believe there are many recognized consultants as well as experienced black belts and Lean senseis that can drive the projects once the program has been selected and implemented.

Chapter 1

The Need for Continuous Improvement

"Continuous improvement is better than delayed perfection" – Mark Twain

Consider this scenario that could happen to either one of us when we are delivering training. It is already 7 a.m., and I am already late for the 8 a.m. week long Six Sigma black belt training that I am conducting! My wife is travelling, which means that I need to drop my son off on the way to his school and then drive to my office. By the time I reach the office and make it to the training room, it is 8.15 a.m. and the trainees are already in the classroom and waiting expectantly for the trainer. I make some apologies about the traffic and the reason behind my delay and make a note to myself to be on time the next day. As I am done for the day, I try to retrace my steps and understand what caused me to wake up at 7 a.m. even though my alarm was set at 6.30 a.m., which was the real root cause for my being late. When I return home the first thing I do is to check my alarm clock. I find that there was a brief power outage the night before that reset my clock and as a result also the alarm! Lesson learned–never depend on an old alarm clock that runs only on electric power and does not have a battery backup. So, from next time onwards I will make sure to have a backup alarm set on my cell phone or discard my current clock and purchase another alarm clock that runs on battery whenever there is a power outage.

Now, the readers might be wondering why we started with the above example. Well that is because this example forms the essence of what continuous improvement is all about. Let us revisit this basic process of coming to the office. What are the requirements, what are the expectations from my perspective as a trainer (note: the expectations can differ from the trainees' perspective though)? A requirement would be to reach the office on time (note: on time would have different definition from one individual to another depending on the time of job, and we will not get into the details. For now let's assume on time is when you need to be in the office). An expectation would be to have a hassle free trip to the office, e.g. not stalled in traffic. And in order to achieve the requirement we will have to ensure that we have a smooth and standard process in the morning and prevent any out-of-normal situations to the extent possible. Of course there is no way we can predict a medical emergency in the morning for example or an accident that shuts down a major highway. However, when it comes to the alarm clock we can plan ahead and ensure that there is built in redundancy in the process, basically error proofing the process. From a trainee's perspective, in this case hopefully their expectation is the same–to have the training started at the scheduled time, which means the trainer should be present a few minutes before the start time to get set up with the material. The moment we start thinking about what we need to do to ensure consistent outcomes and meet our targets we are on the path of applying continuous improvement to our process.

Let us take another example that almost all readers would be familiar with, irrespective of which country they might be living in–the process of home delivery of food or material. As a customer, when you place an order for home delivery you have certain requirements as well as expectation of the product that is being delivered. A few of the key attributes are quality (quality is measured variously but at a very minimum should meet the specifications of what you were expecting), and on-time delivery within a plus or minus window of what the home delivery company promised you at the time of taking the order.

This is the concept of variability and as long as you receive the product you ordered within that window, you are happy. But what if the company misses the window and delivers either too early or late? Either way you are potentially dissatisfied because you might not be ready to receive the delivery or wasting your time waiting for the delivery. So, even if the company *on average* has an extremely good record of delivering around the committed time, in reality they might be delivering order A early and order B late, which would make the average right at the middle! However, the customers who placed the orders A and B will fill the variation and not the average.

A company that is customer focused will try to understand the root cause of this variability and make sure that their window around the committed time of delivery is met almost always, this is the concept of reducing variability and centering the process of home delivery around the committed time. Six Sigma and Lean work on this premise of reducing wastes in the process to make it more efficient and identifying and eliminating root causes to make it less variable.

Now let us take this a step further and consider the experience of ordering a home delivery of a service instead of a physical product. A relatively common example would be when you go on-line or use your TV remote to order a pay-per-view movie or game. Imagine you order a pay-per-view movie, complete all your chores, and sit down in front of the TV and click on your remote only to find that what you ordered was not what you are viewing! Granted this is an extreme example and not likely to happen, but hopefully readers get the point we are trying to make here. With service delivery it gets more difficult to satisfy customers because customers do not have the option of returning the product and getting a replacement product. In most cases the service has to get consumed and even though for some type of services the customer might get refunded for a bad service experience the negative impact on customer satisfaction is usually much stronger compared to when it is a physical product. An exception would be when the customer has the flexibility to defer the consumption of the service for another time. Many readers might have seen the media reports around Carnival Cruise's Splendor that set out for a seven day luxury cruise in late 2010. A fire in the ship's engine room left the ship powerless and the cruise never got completed. The fire resulted in the passengers being stuck in the ship for three days without air conditioning, clean water, or working toilets. An almost similar incident happened recently in 2011 with the MSC Opera cruise ship that left the ship adrift in the Baltic Sea for three days and passengers likewise had to go without clean toilets and face food shortages and lack of hot water. In both the above cases the customers were purchasing a service, a cruise vacation in this case.

As we mentioned previously, the customer dissatisfaction with a service that does not meet the expectation or requirement is significantly higher compared to the dissatisfaction with a product. Even though in both the cases the cruise company gave a full refund and a free voucher, it might not be possible for many customers to plan for another vacation and take a free cruise within the time frame the vouchers are valid. In other words the customer had to consume the service and cannot avail of the replacement service. Plus for many customers the cruise might have been in celebration of a special occasion (anniversary, honeymoon etc.) which is not going to happen again. To prevent these kinds of *defects* in services or to keep them to as low as possible, many large companies in the Services sector globally have started deploying continuous improvement programs. And this is why Lean and Six Sigma has taken off in the banking services, IT services, healthcare and hospitality industries to name a few industries in the services area, in addition to the manufacturing sector where it first started and has been thriving successfully for almost two decades now. Hopefully the two cruise companies that we mentioned before do have a good process improvement methodology in place that can help identify the root cause behind the power loss and prevent those in the future.

What we have discussed is just an example of the value a continuous improvement program can bring to its customer. As a customer, your requirements and expectations define what the provider should be providing either in the form of products or services. Likewise all of our customers have similar expectations when it comes to consuming our products or services. And in order to ensure that we are consistently meeting or exceeding our customers' expectations we will need to have some form of continuous improvement program established within our businesses. Today almost all of the best practices frameworks like ITIL, SCOR, CMMI, ISO etc. recommend Lean Six Sigma as the preferred methodology for driving continuous improvement around these frameworks. In Chapter 4 we will get into the details of how Lean and Six Sigma fit with these frameworks.

Why companies need to have a continuous improvement program:

In 1996 Michael Porter came out with his seminal work "What is Strategy?" that was published in the November-December edition of *Harvard Business Review*. In this article he argued that operational effectiveness and strategy are both required for an organization to perform at a higher level. He defined operational effectiveness as "performing similar activities better than rivals perform them" and includes, but is not limited to, efficiency. So, any activity that, for example, reduces defects would enable the company to be efficient in better utilizing its resources.

Even though in the article Porter makes it clear that strategy is ultimately what will make a company survive in the long run and differentiate it from its competitors, he also states that operational effectiveness is required for companies to survive in the first place. Continuous improvement is needed for the firm to perform similar activities better that will enable the firm to provide higher level of quality and service at a much faster rate compared to the competition. And this is why methodologies like Lean, Six Sigma or Total Quality

Management get deployed. However, as companies deploy continuous improvement programs, they need to be aware of the fact that operational effectiveness cannot supplant strategy. Even as these companies improve their operational effectiveness, they at the same time, should be looking to deliver a different set of values to their customers based on a different set of activities as compared to the rest of the players in the same field–and this is where continuous improvement as a strategy becomes important. For example, selective application of tools like Quality Function Deployment and House of Quality or different ideation tools can help a company uncover innovative ideas that can lead to breakthrough products. Unfortunately, even after fifteen years of publication of the article we come across many companies that are operating at a sub-optimal level of operational effectiveness and are actually ripe for deployment of continuous improvement initiatives and to realize the benefits.

An almost similar argument was made by Gary Hamel in his blog in the *Wall Street Journal* in 2009 titled "Why Companies Fail," though his position is that strategy ultimately dies and it gets replicated or supplanted. However, in order for companies in any field to be the leader, they will need to have a continuous improvement program. Hamel though warns that even though continuous improvement creates an "ultra-efficient business system" for the leader, there is a risk of the company becoming inflexible and not open to innovations which ultimately will kill the company. As we will see in Appendix 1, the problem probably lies in the understanding of which continuous improvement methodology fits best with the culture of a company and applying the tools accordingly.

In order for any company to reach the ultimate frontier of efficiency and effectiveness, and in order to deliver according to customer expectations in the best possible manner (lower costs, high quality, high speed) it needs to have a continuous improvement program that will ultimately make processes highly optimized. As we will see in the next chapter most of the leading companies today, that make it to different top ten lists globally, have a formal continuous improvement program in place.

Let us now take a look at some of the most commonly adopted continuous improvement methodologies:

Plan-Do-Check-Act:

Plan-Do-Check-Act cycle, more commonly known as PDCA cycle, was developed by Walter Shewhart as a continuous improvement process that can supplement the Statistical Quality Control methodology. The PDCA cycle was, however, popularized by Deming who introduced it to Japan after World War II and is commonly referred to as the Deming cycle. As the name suggests, PDCA is a four step process:

In the *plan* stage you establish what you want to accomplish and also establish the metrics and measurement system that can help you verify whether you have been able to accomplish what you set out for.

In the *do* stage you carry out or "do" what you have planned. This is the step where the actual work happens.

In the *check* phase you compare using the measurement system that you have put in place, how you are progressing towards meeting your accomplishment and analyze any deviations.

In the *act* phase deviations are analyzed and solutions implemented to ensure they do not happen again in the future and the gains are standardized. This is also the phase where a debrief or lessons learned exercise is carried out.

PDCA cycle is one of the oldest forms of continuous improvement methodology and almost all of today's improvement methodologies, most prominently Six Sigma and

Lean, are based on the PDCA approach. However, even after all these years, many companies are still struggling to fully understand and successfully deploy this basic methodology primarily when it comes to having a formal "check" and "act" process in place.

Lean:

Lean Methodology focuses on empowering team members to simplify processes and identify non-value added process steps. These steps are then either eliminated or automated to reduce human involvement and improve cycle time. The focus with Lean is to reduce defects and eliminate waste from the process. The Lean thought process has been covered in the book *The Machine that Changed the World* by Womack and Jones. Primarily there are four basic notions of Lean that have been identified [1]:

Lean as a fixed state or goal (*Being Lean*) – This is similar to the concept of being a Six Sigma company where companies set the ideal of being recognized and embraced as a Lean corporation as the ultimate goal.

Lean as a continuous change process (*Becoming Lean*) – This is where an organization identifies and applies Lean methodology relentlessly as a continuous change or improvement approach with the goal of identifying and eliminating all wastes from the process and delivering as per customer demand a defect free product or service.

Lean as a set of tools or methods (*Doing Lean / Toolbox Lean*) – Here Lean is more of a tool rather than a company's culture or way of doing continuous improvement. A typical example would be where a team is working on improving a process and would apply some elements of Lean, like Value Stream Mapping, to identify steps that can be eliminated from the process.

Lean as a philosophy (*Lean Thinking*) – This is probably the most difficult to achieve for an organization. The whole culture of the organization needs to change so that Lean becomes the way the employees do their work and Lean gets embedded as a philosophy within the company.

The book *Lean Transformation* by Bruce Henderson and Jorge Larco lays out the Lean Fundamentals towards transforming a process or organization into a Lean process. The first step of Lean starts with mapping the process for the area that needs to be transformed into Lean. Once this is completed, the area is cleaned, organized, and all items that are not needed for the production process, or service, are removed from the area. Next, continuous flow of material or information is installed and then a Kanban pull scheduling system is implemented to link production to customer order cadence. Setup times and batch sizes are then reduced and any defects in the manufacturing process are removed through root-cause identification and problem solving. Thereby the end goal of defect free parts flowing from the suppliers to the customers in accordance with customers demand is achieved.

Kaizen / Gemba Kaizen:

Kaizen is a term that was coined by Masaki Imai who founded the Kaizen Institute. The Kaizen Institute still holds the copyright to the term "Kaizen" and "Gemba Kaizen." The Kaizen Institute defines Kaizen as "a Japanese term meaning change for the better." When applied to business organizations it implies continual improvement "involving everyone that does not cost much, if any, money". In practical terms, Kaizen is a continuous improvement methodology that focuses on one particular business area that needs improvement. These are usually three to five day events where team members come together and use Lean tools like value stream mapping, Lean opportunity mapping, FMEA, and so forth to identify waste and improvement opportunities. At the end of the event, the team presents solutions to the project sponsor and gets a go/no go decision to implement the solutions. Usually the Kaizen leader sets up a thirty, sixty, and ninety day follow up to keep leadership informed on progress and the project closes within ninety days.

Gemba Kaizen is pretty similar to Kaizen events. The major difference between the two is that Gemba Kaizen focuses on the shop floor where the work is actually being performed. Gemba literally means "the real place" in Japanese. In that sense there can be an IT help desk kaizen, a warehouse kaizen, an engineering design kaizen, and so on.

Hoshin Kanri:

Even though Hoshin Kanri, or "Policy Deployment" as it is sometimes called, is considered a PDCA, Lean, or TQM tool, it is actually quite similar to the common concept of Management By Objective (MBO). However, it is important to note that Hoshin is not same as the MBO approach. The Japanese adopted the Management By Objectives concept plus Deming's Plan-Do-Check-Act cycle and modified them into what is now popularized as Hoshin Kanri. What Hoshin Kanri does is to help an organization identify and focus on the critical few initiatives that need to be undertaken in support of the strategic objective. As per the book *Hoshin Kanri: Policy Deployment for Successful TQM* it is defined as follows: "[Hoshin Kanri] provides a step-by-step planning, implementation, and review process for managed change. Specifically, it is a systems approach to management of change in critical business process [sic]." The book further states, "What hoshin [sic] provides is a planning structure that will bring selected critical business processes up to the desired level of performance." Since Hoshin Kanri follows a very structured approach of tracking the progress of the initiative and owners are made responsible for each critical initiative it ultimately helps a company drive successful results. Note that Hoshin Kanri can be a powerful approach to identifying the most impactful Six Sigma or Lean projects that directly affect a company's strategic goals and making sure that progress is reviewed at the right level and with the right cadence. This also helps those projects get the right level of corporate sponsorship and in turn ensures success of the continuous improvement program.

Hoshin Plan Elements

(adapted from *Hoshin Handbook* by Pete Babich)

- Business Fundamentals Plan – documents daily work and describes what the business is, for an organization based on its mission.

- Long Range Plan – documents how the organization expects to operate in the future. This plan describes what the business should be based on the organization's long term vision.

- Annual Plan – documents the key objectives that need to be accomplished in a given year to ensure the organization is moving on the right track towards achieving the long range plan and vision. This plan documents what the business will be.

- Review Tables – are used to compare actual results versus expected results and document any changes to the plan. Review tables make the plan a living document.

- Abnormality Tables – document any occurrence that is outside the normal range of variation and facilitates root cause identification and implementation of corrective actions.

Six Sigma:

In the book *The Six Sigma Way*, Six Sigma is defined as "a comprehensive and flexible system for achieving, sustaining, and maximizing business success." In essence Six

Sigma is an approach to improve processes and reduce variation, so that customers get near perfect products or services with as little variation as possible. There are two approaches to Six Sigma application, namely DMAIC and DMADV

DMAIC – is an acronym for Define, Measure, Analyze, Improve, and Control. Each of these are stages in the process improvement methodology. Readers might notice how closely the five steps fit with the PDCA cycle. This is because the DMAIC methodology was based on the PDCA cycle. This methodology is applied to existing processes, or in other words processes that are in place but not operating at an optimal level or the process is producing defects. In the *define* phase the voice of customer is collected, the project charter is put together, scope is finalized, the process performance goal or target is established, and the project team is formed. In the *measure* phase, the team brainstorms the potential root causes and comes up with the plan to collect the data that would be needed to track the project performance goal and establishes the baseline and the root causes data. Once the data is collected, the team moves to the *analyze* phase to identify the vital few root causes through extensive statistical analysis, if needed. The team then identifies creative solutions to validate the potential root causes and implements them in the *improve* phase. Once the improvements are validated and the project performance goals are met, a *control* plan is drafted and controls put in place to ensure the improved process is stabilized.

DMADV – is an acronym for Define, Measure, Analyze, Design, and Validate. This methodology is applied where processes do not exist. A perfect example would be when a company is planning to launch a new product which they have never done before. DMADV is also called DFSS or Design For Six Sigma, since the goal of this methodology is to design a process that will be able to deliver products or services at a six sigma level, less than four defects per million products produced. It is important to note that in many cases the six sigma goal is a hypothetical target, in that companies might not want to design a process at such a high defect free level. Designing and maintaining processes to sustain outputs at such high yield levels might not always make business sense. DMADV follows a more rigorous approach compared to DMAIC, and it usually takes longer to complete DMADV projects.

The following table gives a quick comparison between Lean and Six Sigma, note that the last element is common to both Lean and Six Sigma. They both require a change in leadership and employee mindset in order to become a successful and sustainable program.

	Six Sigma	Lean
Differences	Focuses on reducing process variation	Focuses on eliminating waste and reducing cycle time
	Primary goal is to reduce defects in the process output	Primary goal is to reduce non value add or wasteful process steps
	Based on statistical formula that measures the impact of root causes on the process output	Based on best practices
	Data Driven	Observation Driven
	Change in mindset of leadership and employees needed (Six Sigma thinking)	Change in mindset of leadership and employees needed (Lean thinking)

Case Study:

Starwood Hotels and Resorts, North America has built a reputation for being one of the best places to work for Six Sigma professionals globally. In fact they were able to retain the top spot for 2011 in iSixSigma Live! Summit & Awards in Miami from among the annual list of companies nominated. They are the only company in the hospitality industry who have a formal Lean Six Sigma program since 2002.

In 2007 an article appeared in *Businessweek* that describes the problem and opportunity statement for a particular process that Starwood was looking to improve. As the article states, "In January 2006, the Westin Chicago River North hotel was picked to pilot a project, dubbed Unwind, for the upscale hotel chain. The purpose: to imagine a set of nightly activities that would draw guests out of their rooms and into the lobby where they could meet, mingle, and develop a greater loyalty to the hotel group. Westin spied an opportunity with Unwind after a study it produced found 34 percent of frequent travelers feel lonely away from home." Since the hotel chain already had a well established Six Sigma program, they could pull in their team of black belts and green belts to further explore this unique concept. A team was formed consisting of one black belt and four green belts along with other subject matter experts from room service, food and beverage, and sales to brainstorm and identify opportunities. You should note this is a great example where continuous improvement has been used as a tool to come up with an innovative product or service and shows that if properly applied, Six Sigma does not stifle innovation. The outcome of the brainstorming session was to come up with the idea of providing a massage service for the hotel guests to unwind at the end of the day. Using just this thought as a starting point, the team figured out the logistics, location, and so forth and did a dry run. This dry run helped them identify and resolve some potential failure modes with the concept, and then the Six Sigma team handed it over to the process owner who, in this case, was the Fitness Director. As a result of implementing this solution, revenues at the spa went up by as much as 30 percent. This idea was subsequently implemented at multiple locations and the Green Belts helped in setting up a measurement system to track results.

This is a great example of how a proper continuous improvement initiative can help companies think outside the box and actually identify additional ways to further satisfy their customers, increase customer loyalty, and create additional sources of revenue.

Chapter 2

How Relevant is Six Sigma and Lean Today?

"Everything can be improved" – Clarence W. Barron, President Dow Jones Company 1912-1928

"Nature does constant Value Stream Mapping –It's called evolution" – Carrie Latet, Poet

Is Six Sigma and Lean still relevant in 2012 and in the future? Or is continuous improvement just a fad and does not really help companies improve their operations and processes? In order to get some additional insight that might help us answer the first question, we wanted to find out whether continuous improvement is still considered important for businesses and what kind of skill sets companies are looking for to drive continuous improvement projects. For this study we decided to look at two countries–USA and India. There are a couple of reasons behind selecting these two countries. First, we are both pretty familiar with the corporate culture and work ethics having lived and worked in both the countries. Second, we were trying to find a combination of two countries–one country that has moved far along the path of deploying Six Sigma and Lean in most areas and at the same time has been experiencing low GDP growth versus another country where the concepts are still being tentatively tried out and are embraced by a relatively small minority while being one of the fastest growing economies in the last few years. In May 2011 a single search using the keywords "Six Sigma" in the exclusively for over

$100,000 salary job site Ladders.com yielded 800 results; the keyword "Lean" turned up 600 jobs. Things have not changed much since then. In January 2012 there were more than 630 Six Sigma jobs and 650 Lean jobs posted. So this clearly shows the demand for Lean Six Sigma professionals in the industry has remained very high even in these challenging economic conditions. We saw the same pattern in India. In January 2012 we got over 1250 and over 680 results respectively for "Six Sigma" and "Lean" when we searched Naukri.com, which is one of the most popular job sites in India. These results were comparable with the results we got in the previous months.

Now let us address the first question that we asked at the beginning of this chapter. Recently there have been some questions around how effective Six Sigma and Lean approaches are as continuous improvement methodology. The most common and high profile examples that critics of Lean Six Sigma bring up are of 3M and Home Depot. In both companies Lean Six Sigma was launched with tremendous visibility but ultimately had to be rolled back as the methodology was apparently not right for the company. The story of 3Ms failure and our analysis of what went wrong is covered later in this book. While researching for this book, we looked at a few lists of companies excelling in different areas, instead of just focusing on revenue growth, to see if we could find enough evidence of the top companies using Lean, Six Sigma, or Lean Six Sigma as a continuous improvement methodology. First we looked at Gartner's list of Top Supply Chain Companies for 2011. Apple is an exception, as we found no information in the public domain of a Lean Six Sigma program existing within Apple. However, many operations managers and supplier quality leads within Apple have Lean Six Sigma backgrounds and the authors believe the basic concepts of a Lean Six Sigma methodology are being applied at Apple to some degree within the supply chain / quality functions.

The Gartner Supply Chain Top 25 for 2011

Rank	Company	Peer Opinion (25%)	Gartner Opinion (25%)	Three-Year Weighted ROA (25%)	Inventory Turns (15%)	Three-Year Weighted Revenue Growth (10%)	Composite Score
1	Apple	2,950	536	17.9%	49.3	40.9%	8.50
2	Dell	1,909	457	6.6%	38.9	4.1%	5.14
3	P&G	1,726	660	9.6%	5.6	2.4%	5.13
4	Research In Motion (RIM)	550	215	25.1%	17.7	43.9%	5.10
5	Amazon	2,267	402	6.6%	11.2	34.0%	5.07
6	Cisco Systems	1,501	550	10.2%	11.8	5.5%	4.82

Source: Gartner (June 2011)

The next list was the 2010 *Bloomberg Businessweek* "Top 10 Technology Companies" in the world. Once again we found that six out of the top ten technology companies have a very strong and publicized Lean Six Sigma program, as we discussed earlier Apple was one of the exceptions. We are pretty confident that if we were to carry out a similar review of the top five companies globally by revenue, we will pretty much arrive at a similar conclusion. We believe these results would prove to the business leader that Lean and Six Sigma are still very relevant as a Continuous Improvement tool.

Rank	Name	Revenue	Revenue Growth	Operating Income	Shareholder Return
2	Apple	$42.90 billion	14%	$11.74 billion	107%
4	Amazon.com	$24.51 billion	28%	$1.13 billion	70%
5	TCS	$6.1 billion	8%	$1.45 billion	150%
6	Priceline.com	$2.34 billion	24%	$471 million	170%
7	CenturyLink	$4.97 billion	91%	$1.23 billion	37%
8	Cognizant	$3.28 billion	16%	$618 million	106%
9	Infosys	$4.75 billion	15%	$1.41 billion	84%

Top IT Companies, 2010 Bloomberg

In our opinion, one of the reason we still see a lot of skeptics is because of the belief that Lean Six Sigma is just a cost cutting tool; however, that cannot be further from the truth. Lean Six Sigma when properly applied, increases customer and employee satisfaction and have "soft cost" benefits that business leaders don't always see or sometimes even want to see. If cost cutting becomes the end goal for business and the only reason why Six Sigma or Lean is deployed, then chances are these methodologies are going to become irrelevant. Unfortunately too many business leaders' exposure to quality evolution has been limited to experiencing Six Sigma and Lean being used as tools to cut costs. This belief points to the fact that a significant gap in knowledge exists at the senior leadership level about Six Sigma.

For a minute let us keep Six Sigma, Lean, BPM or any other continuous improvement methodology aside and focus on a real life business problem faced by a company that needed to be resolved and the approach taken to address it. A leading global IT services company was missing customer Service Level Agreements (SLAs) related to restoration of critical outages that were impacting the customers. This was causing significant customer dissatisfaction, led to missed Service Level Agreement penalties, and was a leading cause behind customers leaving the company. In order to address this problem, a team of cross functional subject matter experts was formed, led by a dedicated resource to identify the root causes behind the missed SLAs. The first thing the team did was to get everyone together in a room for a two day session to set the scope, charter, and map the end to end process from when a customer experiences an outage to when the outage gets restored. Once the mapping was done, the team could easily identify redundant process steps that were either unnecessary or not optimized. The team also figured out two major issues right upfront–there was no uniform definition around what constituted the correct SLA (start point and end point for measuring the SLA), as well as a lack of a measurement system to track the SLA. The next step for the team was to baseline the existing process metrics and use the data to carry out further analysis to identify the root causes behind the missed SLAs. After the root causes were validated using a combination of graphs, statistical analysis, and team sessions the team went ahead and identified and implemented solutions. Once the solutions started showing the improvements, the team then updated all processes, policies, procedure documents, and established a metric that is reviewed by senior management at least monthly. This led to a decrease in SLA violations by 70 percent. The chart below shows data for the two stages of the project: Stage 1 was before the project was launched, and Stage 2 is after the completion of the project. The Y axis measures the proportion of customer outages that missed the restoration target and the X axis denotes the months the data was pulled.

Proportion of Calls That Missed Restoration Target

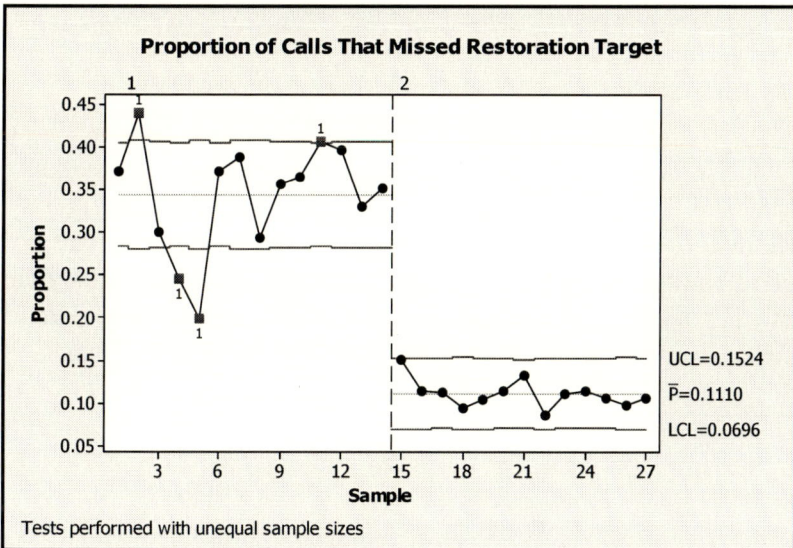

UCL=0.1524
P̄=0.1110
LCL=0.0696

Tests performed with unequal sample sizes

Is this an approach that the company would probably like to take in future again to solve business problems? The answer hopefully for most readers would be an emphatic yes! And if the answer is yes, Six Sigma, Lean, BPM or any other such structured improvement methodology for driving process improvement will always remain relevant, in future they might be called by a different name though! Now let's go back to the example of the IT services company that was missing SLAs related to timely restoration of critical customer impacting outages. What the team actually applied to address the issue was a combination of Lean and Six Sigma tools and methodology. The team started by finalizing the charter (define phase tool from Six Sigma), did a Value Stream Mapping to identify wastes (Lean tool), established metrics and measurement system (measure phase tool from Six Sigma), analyzed data to identify root causes and implemented solution (analyze and improve phase tools from Six Sigma as well as Lean tools to identify opportunities). Once the solutions were implemented and working, the team ensured that the metric and measurement was added to a top level corporate dashboard and updated the documents and processes (control phase of Six Sigma). So, as we can see from this example, any process improvement can and will continue in the future to use elements of the established process improvement framework that have been tried and proven, and these approaches will always remain relevant.

We have mentioned earlier in the book that recently some critics of Lean and Six Sigma have been citing Toyota's quality challenges as proof of the fact that these methodologies are not good enough to prevent or reduce defects. However, an article titled "Lean Manufacturing's Next Life" by David Drickhammer in *ChiefExecutive.Net* on March 2010 makes it very clear that, in spite of the negative press that Toyota has been receiving for the last couple of years because of quality issues and safety recalls, the Lean manufacturing methodology that was pioneered by Toyota is here to stay. *ChiefExecutive.Net* is a web magazine for the CEO and CXO community. We also firmly believe what Toyota needs is to refocus internally on the methodologies it developed and popularized, if they are to get to the root cause of the issues they face.

With the current challenging economic conditions we have also seen most global organizations have to improve their productivity and get the same work done with fewer resources, compared to before 2008. In addition companies are automating or off-shoring many of their processes. In these situations it becomes even more imperative for companies to have a strong process improvement methodology in place that can help leadership make the right decisions by highlighting wastes and non-value added activities, reducing process variation, and standardizing processes that can be relatively easily automated or off-shored. Our belief is that the progress we have seen in the continuous improvement world is here to stay and the basic concepts of Lean and Six Sigma, as well as other methodologies that have been discussed in this book, will be very much in demand. Our recommendation to business leaders struggling to meet customer demand would be to go down the path of deploying a structured continuous improvement program to help identify what are the customer needs and be able to align their internal business processes around that need.

As we will see in the next chapter, most of the process improvement models including ITIL (used extensively in the IT service industry), SCOR and CMMI actually support using Six Sigma and Lean as process improvement tools. The approach and tools behind Six Sigma and Lean will remain relevant in the future. However, it is important to note that generally the skill set requirement around Lean, Six Sigma, or BPM has changed and are now complementary to other business competencies such as business management, project management, change management and so forth. The reason behind this is that Six Sigma deployment has evolved from the early stages when it was a new concept and the ones who were trained early became specialists who were sought for their knowledge. Since then pure Six Sigma or Lean knowledge has become more of a commodity and additional skills are expected from a continuous improvement practitioner in addition to a Lean or Six Sigma certification to successfully meet and deliver on business expectations.

Case Study:

Around the time we were writing this book, the process had already started in the United States for the presidential elections of 2012 and the Republican party was going through the procedure of identifying the challenger to President Obama. However, one very interesting fact that probably did not get as much coverage in the popular press as it deserved was the pledge that most of the Republican contenders took to reduce wastes in how the Government operates and reduce the national debt by applying the principles of Lean Six Sigma. This movement was started by Mike George, a Texas-born business consultant who founded Strong America Now and believes in Lean Six Sigma as the best methodology that can help the US Government systematically identify and eliminate wasteful spending and thereby bring Government spending under control without having to cut any programs or raising taxes. Strong America Now estimated that up to $500 billion in savings could be achieved annually by identifying and reducing 25 percent of wasteful Government spending. In a report that appeared in *TheGazette.com*, George said "[T]the effort likely would mean a reduction in force because so much Government spending is personnel costs associated with people doing tasks that likely are not needed to conduct an efficient, streamlined operation that focuses on the best way to achieve desired outcomes." As of January 2012, five of the seven republican contenders remaining in the running have already signed a pledge to utilize Lean Six Sigma methodology if they were elected to the White House. This is in addition to two pledged Republican candidates who pulled out of the race in late 2011.

It is important to mention here that the US Government already has a very successful Six Sigma program running within the Department of Defense which is managed by the Lean Six Sigma Program Office. In a report published on September 2008, the program office highlights a few successful projects that were completed including one that earned the Shingo Prize for Excellence in Manufacturing (Silver Medallion). This project called "Heavy Expanded Mobility Tactical Truck (HEMTT)" resulted in reduction of cycle time by 75 percent, reduction in rework by 51 percent and exceeded delivery requirements of assets. Another project that was a recipient of the Malcolm Baldridge National Quality

Award resulted in cost benefit/avoidance of several millions of dollars over six years!

The very fact that most of the presidential contenders of the largest economy in the world are proposing Lean Six Sigma as a methodology to solve the biggest problem facing the American economy in decades combined with the fact that Lean Six Sigma is already widely applied in different governmental departments shows the power of the methodology. There can probably be no stronger statement on the future of Lean Six Sigma as an extremely proven continuous improvement tool!

Chapter 3

Choosing the Right Continuous Improvement Methodology – Lean or Six Sigma?

"If you don't know where you are going, you will probably end up somewhere else." ~Lawrence J. Peter, Educator, Hierarchiologist, and the founder of The Peter Principle

As the title of the chapter suggests, we decided to focus on Lean and Six Sigma since these are the two most adopted continuous improvement methodologies. However, we think this chapter will also help leaders who are planning to deploy other continuous improvement methodologies to follow a similar approach.

Many companies ask themselves the question – are we ready to embrace Lean or Six Sigma methodology and struggle with the answer. Unfortunately there is no easy answer. In *The Six Sigma Way*, Pande et al suggest that companies thinking of embarking down this path should first look at three key areas to assess their readiness: assess outlook and future path, evaluate current performance, and review systems and capacity for change and improvement. The findings to these key areas will hopefully give companies a better sense for their readiness to deploy. Having said that, one thing that the book does say is that if there is already a successful performance and process improvement methodology in place, implementing a formal Lean or Six Sigma program might actually confuse the people.

Additionally Six Sigma does call for substantial investments and if there is no significant business outcome that can be estimated, it will be difficult to support the program. Lean, however, can be implemented with relatively fewer resources and time commitment and can become a good continuous improvement methodology to deploy to get some quick wins that can help build the business justification for deploying a full-fledged Lean Six Sigma program in future.

Many continuous improvement efforts have failed because of a one-size fits all approach. The continuous improvement methodology needs to fit in with the overall goals of the business as well as the specific project goals. Two important factors need to be kept in mind while identifying the proper methodology.

1.   Does the selected methodology fit in with the overall business vision and strategy (*Strategic Approach*)?

2.   Does the selected methodology make sense based on the type of business problem we are trying to solve (*Framework Approach*)?

Strategic Approach:

Unless the selected continuous improvement methodology fits within an organization's strategic and business goals there is little chance of generating breakthrough results. It also should fit in with senior leadership's experience and understanding of the particular methodology. In the bestseller *Straight From the Gut*, Jack Welch talks about how GE considered a Deming program and ruled it out as a companywide initiative because Jack Welch felt it was too theoretical. However, when GE decided to go for Six Sigma because an internal survey said that "quality was a problem at GE," Jack, in his own words, "went nuts about Six Sigma and launched it." He also went on to say that, "when we decided to go forward (with Six Sigma), we did so with a vengeance."

Like all successful business transformation initiatives, depending on the selected methodology, a program needs to be put in place as well as ensure that the program is staffed with the proper resources. The lack of proper support structure with a PMO to select and manage projects can lead to a quick demise of any continuous improvement initiative. Likewise a company that chooses Lean/Kaizen methodology as the continuous improvement tool needs to ensure there are a few trained Lean/Kaizen leaders on board before rolling out any improvement methodology. The authors have experienced firsthand the pit falls of not having the right mentoring/coaching infrastructure in place and the sole dependence on external consultants to train black belts and expect successful results.

When to Use Lean and When to Use Six Sigma:

Generally speaking from a strategic perspective, a company that is growing will be more successful using Six Sigma whereas a company more focused on eliminating wastes and cutting costs would benefit more quickly from a Lean program and specifically targeted Kaizen events. Refer to the table that identifies the preferred methodology based on the Organization's Key Objective. Since Lean is less data analysis intensive and based more on team based subject matter expert anecdotal process improvement, it usually allows only a fraction of the total improvement potential to be achieved. Six Sigma takes it to the next level, though it takes longer to achieve those benefits. DFSS is usually introduced when the company has matured enough with the Lean and DMAIC Six Sigma approach.

Organization's Key Objective or Situation	Lean / Kaizen or Six Sigma
Focus on quick results	Lean (Six Sigma projects usually take between three to six months on average)
Focus on cutting costs	Lean or Kaizen projects usually result in a reduction in process steps as well as overall costs associated with a process
Delivering very low defect rate of product or service	Six Sigma – by its very definition a Six Sigma process will have only 3.4 defects per million products
Reduce variation from key process and outputs	Six Sigma focuses on reducing variation from a process
Limited data analysts or trained experts capable of carrying out data analysis	Lean – Lean/Kaizen projects usually require far less data and very little statistical analysis
Targeting an IPO in the near future	Lean – a Six Sigma program is usually costlier to sustain and takes longer on average to deliver

It is also important to point out here that some companies consciously decide to avoid the Six Sigma approach and instead focus on utilizing a Lean methodology, and more specifically Kaizen events, for driving continuous improvement. On the other hand there are others who are firm believers in the combined power of Lean and Six Sigma. And then there are still others who take a step approach and would, for example, implement a Lean program before moving on to Six Sigma implementation as the company matures. There is nothing wrong with any of these approaches as long as it supports the overall business strategy. The important thing to remember is that there will always be some projects in every company that can be more successfully driven using a Six Sigma framework instead of Lean and vice versa.

Framework Approach:

Even with the right strategic approach in place some continuous improvement initiatives have failed because of the focus on just one methodology (e.g. all projects are mandated to follow the Six Sigma framework). The reason this does not work is because not all projects require the rigor of Six Sigma or for that matter even a Lean approach. In these companies the continuous improvement initiatives get launched with a lot of fanfare and support, but what eventually happens is that senior leaders soon lose their appetite as they see projects taking longer to complete then initially anticipated or when the projects generate sub-optimal results. There are numerous instances of companies whose leaders have been left with a bad taste for Six Sigma just because these kinds of projects take around six months on average to complete. So, if a project that does not require the rigor of Six Sigma is made to go through the Six Sigma approach, inevitably the leaders or sponsors of the project will start getting frustrated as they wait for the results. Likewise, the results will not be as per the expectations of the sponsors if the Six Sigma methodology is not applied to a project that is complex and could have benefited from the systematic data-based root cause identification and solutions. In order to avoid these kinds of situations there is a simple framework that can be easily applied right at the initiation phase of any major impact project within an organization. Note that the continuous improvement group or department is usually the best positioned to assist other departments in identifying the correct methodology–this is because the MBBs and Lean experts usually reside within this group. We will take the example of a hypothetical medical equipment repair services company which observes high dead-on-arrival (DOA) rates within its spare parts operations to demonstrate how the right improvement methodology can be selected, depending on the issue. It is also important to mention here that it is not mandatory to apply a Six Sigma approach, or any other continuous improvement methodology for that matter, to business problems that would fall in the lower right quadrant. It is just that a Six Sigma approach would, in most cases, generate a much better outcome compared to a non-structured approach to addressing the business problem.

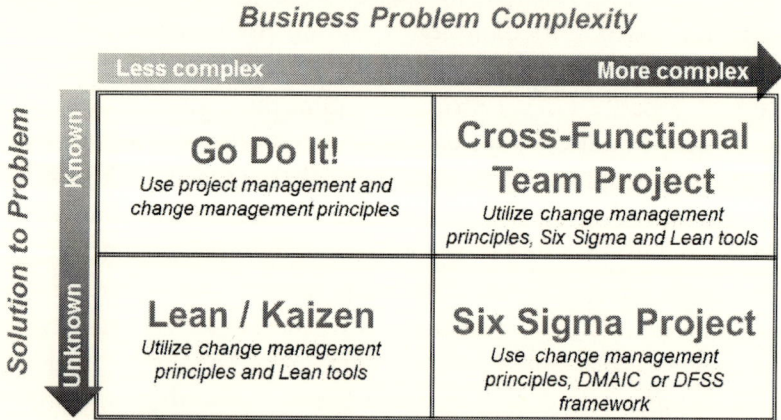

Business Problem Complexity

	Less complex	More complex
Known	**Go Do It!** *Use project management and change management principles*	**Cross-Functional Team Project** *Utilize change management principles, Six Sigma and Lean tools*
Unknown	**Lean / Kaizen** *Utilize change management principles and Lean tools*	**Six Sigma Project** *Use change management principles, DMAIC or DFSS framework*

Solution to Problem

- Go-Do-It:

For a newly launched replacement part which is coming back as DOA pretty frequently there is enough information in the return form that helps the employees identify that the problem the part is getting returned for is not because it is defective, but rather because the customers who depend on installation instructions on the company's web site cannot find anything specific for the new spare part. The employees know the return rate can be reduced by providing end users with better installation instructions on the company web site. This problem has a known fix and requires implementation of the corrective action. If the solution is already known and the project is not complex, it is better to run the project as a GDI initiative. There is no point trying to Lean the process or, even worse, apply the full Six Sigma DMAIC rigor to such projects. Applying DMAIC or Lean will unnecessarily tie up valuable resources and increase customer dissatisfaction with the spare part (and reverse logistics costs).

- Cross Functional Team Workshops:

For the newly launched spare part, the employees know that the DOA return rate can be reduced by providing some end users with better installation instructions. However, the team needs to first analyze the data and understand which type of customers are returning the parts more because of lack of appropriate instructions. Approval from legal and assurance that the instructions meet sustainability requirements will also be required before sharing the instructions with the customers. Plus input of field service engineers is needed to decide the most effective way to share the revised instructions with the customers. In this instance a cross functional team is required that will get together to define the solution and possibly use appropriate Six Sigma tools to stratify the data to come up with the most impactful solutions (e.g. in this particular case the team might make use of Pareto charts to segment the returns by type of customers which in turn will help draft a more customer appropriate part replacement / installation instructions).

- Lean / Kaizen Project:

The company observes a high DOA rate for a particular spare part when compared to DOA rates for the rest of the spare parts. In this case the company does not know what the root cause is behind the high DOA return rate. At the same time the problem is not very complex, since the issue is limited to one spare part. This project of reducing the DOA rates for the particular spare part would benefit most from a Kaizen event, which is nothing but a focused Lean session. In this case a group of subject matter experts from different areas will be pulled together (e.g.

engineering, field services, supply chain/logistics, customer etc.) to better understand the process flow, what the potential failure modes are, waste in the process, and what is causing the defect. Once the root cause is identified, the team will develop the proposed corrective action and get senior leadership buy in for implementation of the solution at the end of the Kaizen event.

- Six Sigma DMAIC project:

The company observes a high DOA rate for all spares compared to their industry peers and there is a high level of customer dissatisfaction with the maintenance service because of the high level of DOA rate as experienced by the customer. This is a perfect situation where a Six Sigma DMAIC approach can and should be applied. This is a complex business problem and the solution is not known yet. Extensive analysis will be required to map the process and collect data for in depth study to identify the root causes. A GDI or even Lean Kaizen event will not be appropriate in this case and chances are that without applying the DMAIC framework the outcome from any such workshop will be sub-optimal and the company will find itself in the same position, even after putting in a lot of effort without the right framework.

Case Study:

A couple of years ago a large telecom company was acquired by another company. Both the companies had well established and successful Six Sigma programs in place. However, post-merger there was a change in leadership and a decision was made to dismantle the Six Sigma program and let go of the MBBs and Black Belts. Instead a Lean program was instituted with focus on three-day Kaizen events with senior leaderships committing support and resources. This program has proven to be successful as well but with a different flavor. Even though the company chose to continue with continuous improvement, it changed the approach that had been very successful. Why was the shift made? One of the key focuses of Lean is to reduce waste and eliminate costs quickly and make the enterprise more lean. Post-merger and with the pressure of rising costs and falling revenue amidst the recession the economy was going through, it made more sense to focus on quick surgical events to eliminate costs and reduce waste. These events required fewer resources, time, and analysis and was more focused on identifying opportunities to improve productivity and efficiency without significantly changing the process or going through the time and data intensive root cause analysis the Six Sigma approach called for. A good example was leaning the defective returns to laboratory for analysis process. A Six Sigma approach would have focused on identifying why the products were being returned (root cause behind shipping defective products) and eliminate the root cause and thereby reduce defective returns. The Lean approach was to make the returns process as efficient as possible and eliminate wastes in the return supply chain.

Chapter 4

Continuous Improvement in the ITIL, SCOR, CMMI, PMBOK and ISO World

"Simple, clear purpose and principles give rise to complex intelligent behavior. Complex rules and regulations give rise to simple stupid behavior" – Dee Hock

International Standardization Organization or ISO has been around for many years and a large number of companies across the globe and in multiple industries have been ISO 9000 certified, and recently more companies are going for additional industry specific best in class certifications or frameworks. Understandably there are dozens of such certifications or best practice models out there, and we cannot address all of them in this book. This chapter will cover, in addition to ISO certification, three other major best in class frameworks and study their relationship and relevance with structured continuous improvement programs like Lean and Six Sigma.

Six Sigma and Lean in the ITIL World:

ITIL (Information Technology Infrastructure Library) is a framework for Information Technology Service Management or ITSM and IT Operations. The first set of best in class practices and recommendations were put together in the 1980s by the UK Government's Central Computer and Telecommunications Agency to manage the growth and dependence of IT and to establish a common set of guidelines on IT management, since most companies were creating their own management practices and these were not consistent. The basic format of ITIL is based on a process management approach and is, at times, credited to Deming's PDCA approach. This set of management practices formed the IT Infrastructure Library. The Central Computer and Telecommunications Agency later merged into the Office of Government Commerce under UK Treasury and has been managing the different versions since then. The current version in circulation is ITIL v3. ITIL is increasingly being adopted by companies as the source of good practice in service management and is applicable to all types of organizations that provide services to a business. As per the ITIL handbook, "The service lifecycle is an approach to IT service management that emphasizes the importance of coordination and control across the various functions, processes, and systems necessary to manage the full lifecycle of IT services. The Service Management Lifecycle approach considers the strategy, design, transition, operation, and continuous improvement of IT services." A's we see ITIL focuses extensively on continuous improvement and calls for a separate Continual Service Improvement function as part of the Service Lifecycle. As per ITIL, "Continual Service Improvement is responsible for managing improvements to IT Service Improvement Processes and IT services." In fact the ITIL Continual Services Improvement model is based on the Deming Plan-Do-Check-Act cycle.

The biggest challenge that corporations implementing ITIL have to face is the change management issue that arises when the company needs to restructure to meet the ITIL recommended approach. This, at times, makes it difficult to implement a continuous improvement program simultaneously because of the change management issues that could arise from managing multiple large scale implementations. However, companies that have successfully implemented Six Sigma or Lean programs in conjunction with ITIL have actually leaned on the Continual Service Improvement ITIL best practices and leveraged the streamlined functions that ITIL puts in place along with indentified roles and owners for all major processes. So ITIL implementation can practically help a company in speeding up the acceptance of a structured continuous improvement program.

As per the ITIL Continual Service Improvement guide/handbook a combination of Six Sigma, Lean, and CMMI works best for IT services organizations. Six Sigma is recognized by ITIL as one of the best practices that supports Continuous Service Improvement in the information technology industry. In fact, from the list of *Bloomberg Businessweek* Digital Elite Top 10 IT Companies for 2010, seven have Six Sigma programs or Black Belts in their organization. Listed below are those six companies:

> Apple ranked second, but there is no information readily available whether Apple has a formal Six Sigma program but they have Black Belt certified employees; Amazon (ranked fourth); Tata Consulting Services (ranked fifth); Priceline (ranked sixth); CenturyLink (ranked seventh); Cognizant Technology Services (ranked eighth); and Infosys (ranked ninth), all have Six Sigma programs

Six Sigma and Lean in the SCOR World:

Supply Chain Operations Reference Model (or SCOR) is the world's "most widely accepted framework for evaluating and comparing supply chain activities and their performance." The model was established and is maintained by the Supply Chain Council which is a global non-profit organization made up of "all organizations interested in applying and advancing the state-of-the-art supply chain management systems and practices." Lean Six Sigma is recommended by the Supply Chain Council as a good fit with the continuous improvement requirements for SCOR. In fact, the Supply Chain council provides training specifically on Six Sigma and Lean using SCOR for companies and individuals. The Six Sigma and Lean training using SCOR helps companies that are using or implementing the SCOR framework "extend the benefits of continuous improvement across their extended supply chain to create overall system improvements."

Supply chain which includes sourcing, manufacturing, storing, and delivering and returning of a physical product is one of the process areas where Lean and Six Sigma have been applied for a long time. For the last few years we also have been hearing about a new term called services supply chain. Services Supply Chain considers the value chain that produces a service for the customer. The hotel industry, IT industry, and banking industry are a few examples of companies that have a services supply chain. Lean tools like Value Stream Analysis and Lean Opportunity Mapping can readily be applied to the supply chain and identify waste across the supply chains. Likewise Six Sigma tools like SIPOC as well as the whole DMAIC methodology fits in very well with any process improvement initiative in the supply chain delivery. A great example would be a Lean Six Sigma project focused on increasing on-time delivery to customer requested time and reducing variability to the committed time. Dell is an example of a company that differentiates itself because of its innovative supply chain that is supported by a network of Lean manufacturers. Most of the iPads and iPhones for Apple are manufactured by Foxconn in China. It is no coincidence that Apple gained the top spot as the most valuable global brand in 2011, as well as the number one supply chain company by Gartner for the fourth consecutive year in 2011. Foxconn has a well-entrenched Lean Six Sigma product to ensure that Apple's product meets the high quality requirements that customers expect. A good point to note here is that Apple focuses on innovation and developing products for the future and Foxconn is the supply chain partner to ensure that the products are manufactured and available on time with quality to meet customer demands. As we will see in other chapters, some companies struggle with the application of Lean Six Sigma or any other structured continuous improvement concepts with the innovation process, but it can become a competitive advantage when it is applied to the design, manufacture, and supply of the product that is the output of the innovation process. However, it is important to highlight here that many companies have successfully utilized Six Sigma in the invention or innovation process as well. We have already seen the example of Starwood Hotels in the case study in Chapter 1 where they came up with a first of its kind service to better serve their customer utilizing the Six Sigma team.

Six Sigma and Lean in the CMMI World:

Capability Maturity Model Integration or CMMI is a capability model developed by the Software Engineering Institute (SEI) along with a group of government and industry representatives and is defined as a "non-prescriptive collections of best practices that infuse quality into products through the use of better processes throughout the entire product life cycle." This model is made up of the "best-of-the-best" practices taken from multiple disciplines. As per Wikipedia, "CMMI is a process improvement approach whose goal is to help organizations improve their performance. CMMI can be used to guide process improvement across a project, a division, or an entire organization."

CMMI recommends grouping of business practices into four categories. These categories are Process Management, Project Management, Engineering, and Support. As per a Carnegie Mellon University's Software Engineering Institute technical note, the Process Management process areas provide the framework for institutionalization and consistent execution of processes across an organization. The Project Management process areas cover the project management activities related to planning, monitoring, and controlling projects. The Engineering process areas cover development and maintenance activities that are shared across engineering disciplines and apply to the development of any product or service in the engineering development domain. Finally Support process areas cover the activities that support product development and maintenance.

An article titled "Relationships between CMMI and Six Sigma" published by CMU/SEI in 2006 explores in details the relationship between Six Sigma and CMMI. The article suggests that Six Sigma can be used to implement CMMI process areas by treating them as Six Sigma projects. The key is to identify problems within a process area and go about improving the process using data-based analysis and depending on whether the process already exists, however broken, or whether it is a green field process, DMAIC or DFSS methodology can be applied in conjunction with Lean as needed. The article further states that Six Sigma can be used as a tactical tool for achieving high capability and maturity. This can be done by improving the defined processes that address the high maturity process areas and strive to drive those processes to achieve Six Sigma quality and thereby achieve high maturity.

Six Sigma and Lean in the PMBOK World:

PMBOK stands for Project Management Book of Knowledge and Project Management Professionals (PMPs) are certified as experts in Project Management by the Project Management Institute (PMI). The PMBOK recognizes Six Sigma and Lean Six Sigma as Quality Management Methodologies. The PMBOK recommended tools for performing quality control are pretty much the tools that are used by a Six Sigma or Lean practitioner as well (e.g. cause and effect diagrams, control charts, histogram, Pareto charts, statistical sampling etc.).

The Quality Management Methodologies mentioned in PMBOK include Six Sigma, Lean Six Sigma, and Quality Function Deployment, which is used extensively in design for Six Sigma projects. In fact the PMI recognizes Lean and Six Sigma training while calculating continuing education points necessary for maintaining the PMP certification. We have come across many Six Sigma Belts who are PMP certified as well and this really helps, particularly in managing large projects.

Six Sigma and Lean in the ISO World:

We have come across multiple companies that are ISO certified (ISO 9001, ISO 14000 and ISO 20000 are the most common ones that we have seen). And being part of multiple internal and external audits we have had the opportunity to demonstrate to various auditors Lean and Six Sigma approaches that were being used to drive continuous improvement in these companies. In all cases these methodologies (and the associated process to gather data, analyze data and document and measure improvements) were always cited by the auditors as best in class approaches that supplement the ISO requirements around continuous improvement.

The bottom line is that Six Sigma and Lean not only fits in perfectly with the most widely adopted process improvement standards but is actually recommended by most of them as the preferred approach for driving continuous improvements in companies following these standards or any other similar best practice model.

Case Study:

In 2009 and 2010 a global IT services company had just gone through a massive organizational change to align itself with the ITIL functions. This called for significant change management and restructuring of roles and responsibilities. All the employees of the organization were also made to go through ITIL training and get certified. Once the change was made, the company then focused on building its service improvement function and decided to use Lean Six Sigma as one of the tools to drive continuous improvement projects. Since the company did not have any certified belts in-house, it recruited external resources to start the program. Since then the program has grown within the company and has also been recognized by external ISO20000 auditors (the particular division within the company is ISO20000 certified) as a best in class model of service improvement.

Chapter 5

Build Internal Capability or Hire External Consultants?

"My greatest strength as a consultant is to be ignorant and ask a few questions" – Peter F. Drucker

A leading company decided to embark on the path of implementing a Six Sigma program. The program had the right support and visibility to top leadership and the program was officially run by the quality organization and supported by middle and senior business leaders who made up the steering committee. However, since the company didn't have any in-house resources to establish the program, a reputed external consultant was hired to deliver the training and also set aside a few hours to mentor the newly trained belts on their first project. The initial set of projects was chosen and twelve belts were sent to the training class. However, it soon became apparent the belts were not able to deliver on the projects with a few exceptions. For newly trained belts, one of the most important criteria behind successful Six Sigma project completion is the mentoring process. Since the consultant had only a few hours to support each candidate, it did not work out for the twelve projects. Ultimately only two projects got completed and the initiative died a painful death. Would the company have been more successful in deploying the Six Sigma program if they had focused on building the capacity in-house by hiring external Master Black Belts or Black Belts?

This has been a question that comes up very frequently when businesses and leaders decide to implement a formal continuous improvement program and especially when a decision is made to implement a Six Sigma or Lean methodology based program. In our experience there are no right answers and any organization embarking on a continuous improvement journey needs to assess their current situation and make a decision accordingly. Hopefully the topics that we will address in the reminder of this chapter will help the reader better arrive at the right decision.

External Consultants:

External consultants can help companies figure out which methodology would be best suited for the business issues, based on corporate direction and overall projects. This would prevent companies from building a Six Sigma infrastructure only to find out leadership wants to see quick improvements that are better driven through Kaizen events using Lean tools, or vice versa. External consultants are also best suited when a company needs quick results or wants to apply the benefits of say a DMAIC approach to a strategic initiative and do not have in-house capability. In such instances engaging an external consultant is a more prudent approach.

Hiring resources to start the program external consultants also serve a very important role in identifying and vetting that the right resources are selected for a company that is new to the Six Sigma or Lean world. This becomes more important when the program is driven by a business leader who, it is safe to assume, does have an appreciation of the power of Lean or Six Sigma. Otherwise this leader would not have championed the program at the first place, but he or she might not be knowledgeable enough to ensure he or she is bringing in the right talent to start the program. This is where the consultants with their experience can ensure the candidates that are shortlisted would be able to meet the requirements of the position and the program.

Evaluating consultants: If it makes sense to hire external consultants to start the continuous improvement program, they need to be held to the same performance evaluation measures that an internal business leader or continuous improvement team would be expected to.

A few key questions that need to be answered while doing the performance evaluation of a consultant are listed below.

- Did the consultant understand the business and organization? This cannot be overlooked. Often a consultant without proper industry knowledge or experience may actually kill the enthusiasm of the business leaders to start a continuous improvement program by failing to deliver the expected results.
- Did they avoid confusing jargons? From a change management perspective we have found that keeping it simple usually is the better approach, especially for an organization that has no past history of continuous improvement.
- Did they document the activities? If the end goal of the organization is to build a self-sustaining continuous improvement program, then it is very important to make sure all activities are documented properly. Another important benefit of this is avoiding legal hassles when it comes to paying for the consultants' efforts.
- Did they involve all staff members as needed? This question becomes extremely important in driving change management. Change acceptance is much higher if people are involved in driving change instead of being told to change.
- Did they produce what they were expected to produce and provide the expected benefits from the program? The author's personal experience shows that in order to generate the full benefit from a consultant engagement when starting a continuous improvement program, it makes sense

to set a project completion target for the consultant besides just the training and certification. Of course necessary checks and balances need to be put in place such that the consultant is not penalized if a project fails due to issues beyond the consultant's control.

- Finally, if an organization decides to engage an external consultant to launch their continuous improvement program or even to drive a specific improvement project we would strongly recommend they request past references from the consultant. Unfortunately there is no regulatory body for Six Sigma or Lean certification and in our combined experience in the Lean/ Six Sigma space we have come across quite a few consultants who were not able to deliver upon the promises they made when they took on the consulting engagements.

Factors	Build Internal Capability	Hire External Resources
Resources available or can be hired (Note: External consultants can be engaged to help in ensuring the right resources are hired)	X	
Need to start a program quickly (Note: This can be done both ways. If a MBB or Lean Master is recruited, a program can be started internally pretty quickly as well)	X	X
Business owners have extremely strong bias (Note: External consultants are treated as neutral and can help address the bias)		X

No dedicated resources with time availability		X
Cross functional resistance		X
Faster ROI (Note: usually external consultants can deliver faster ROI on targeted projects. Ramping up internal capability takes longer unless experienced practitioners are hired)		X
Sustainable program, Continuous Improvement as differentiator	X	
Cost cutting		X
Executive visibility to projects (Note: consultants are usually recruited by senior leadership and have direct access to them)		X
Provide training and impart knowledge	X	X
Significant change management required (Note: External consultants are considered neutral and also can bring in executive visibility and support for projects)		X
Mentor / coach role for initial deployment (Note: would need highly experienced resources to do this in-house)		X
Advisor to leadership during roll-out		X

Chart: This chart gives a quick comparison between engaging/ hiring external consultants and an internal continuous improvement program.

Building Internal Capability:

When an organization decides to implement a full-fledged continuous improvement program across the business with visible senior leader support and commitment, it makes better sense to build the capability internally. This sends the right change message to the entire organization as well and shows the business is serious in devoting budget and resources towards building an internal program. In addition an internal program can also serve as a wonderful tool for reducing unwanted employee attrition. If the program is properly monitored and managed, it becomes a vehicle for top employees to move up the organizational ladder by getting trained as Green Belts and Black Belts and even potentially as Master Black Belts. Many companies with a well-recognized internal continuous improvement program have not only benefitted in terms of being able to retain their high performers but also have managed to draw top talents from outside. This, in turn, has helped these companies achieve breakthrough results from their continuous improvement program.

Long Range Sustainability and Building Continuous Improvement in the Organization's Culture:

As we have discussed earlier, utilizing external consultants might be the right option as an organization is starting to build a continuous improvement program. However, if the end goal of the company is to build a long, lasting improvement culture where every employee is empowered and enthused to contribute, putting in place an internal infrastructure is extremely important. Where applicable, consultants can help provide the initial success, push, and help in getting the right resources onboard in the immediate term. These resources then should be tasked with building the internal capability and culture.

Continuous Improvement Program Existing:

Occasionally, even with a successful continuous improvement program in place, it might be more effective for organizations to hire external consultants. One good example that we have seen is for a company that was trying to combine Hoshin Kanri with their well established Lean Six Sigma program. Although the company had many Black Belts and a couple of Master Black Belts, they did not have anyone with in-depth knowledge around Hoshin Kanri deployment. Bringing in an external Hoshin expert actually helped the company realize their goals pretty quickly. Also, it is a good practice to bring in an external consultant at regular intervals. This gives the company an outside perspective, plus the consultant can review the current program status and provide feedback on how it can be improved by comparing the company's approach and practices with other best in class companies and industries.

Resources Available:

In a few large companies we have observed that, for example, two different divisions might have totally different approaches. One division might have a fully staffed and dedicated internal continuous improvement program whereas another division might have a few projects run by external consultants. The biggest fallout of this structure is the lack of knowledge sharing and replication benefits that the company can otherwise realize with an integrated quality program. This is most likely to happen when there is no single senior leader in the CEO staff who is personally championing or leading the quality or continuous improvement organization.

Choosing the Right Deployment Model for Your Organization:

Depending on whether an organization decides to build the program internally or hire external consultants, the deployment model would somewhat vary. However, the diagram below should equally help business leaders in making a decision as to which approach they should be following given the pros and cons and then make the decision to build internal capability or hire external resources based on the decision criteria we have touched upon over the course of this chapter.

Approaches

Pilot Project Approach

Training Approach

PROS
- Entire Value Stream Improvement
- High Impact & High Visibility
- Easy to realize financial and operational improvement

PROS
- Simultaneous improvement in various business areas
- Several people will be trained and capable of driving future improvements
- Easy to get buy-in and easy to engage people

Select a High Impact Product Line and Transform it end to end using Lean Six Sigma Tools

Select Number of Projects in various product lines/areas and select a core group of people to go through a 3 – 4 week Lean Leader or Six Sigma Black Belt program

CONS
- Improvement will be on only one area
- Limited people development.

CONS
- There will be several small improvements.
- Attendees need to be supported well to complete their projects

Assessment

Kick-off

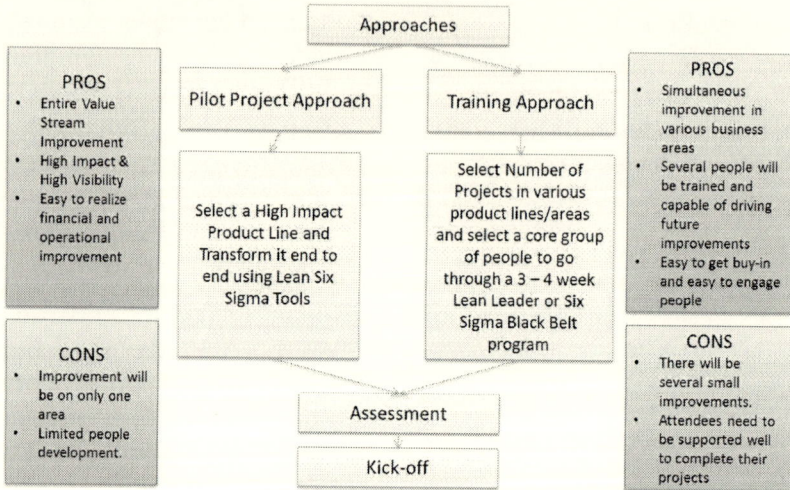

A quick final comment–we have also actually come across organizations where, in spite of building an internal infrastructure, their continuous improvement program failed to take off and the companies had to ultimately resort to engaging external consultants to drive a "stealth" program. In our opinion this can mostly be related back to the change management application or rather the lack of it in these organizations around the continuous improvement program.

Case Study:

A public transportation company in a large US city wanted to redesign their IT strategy for the future. This needed a systematic approach to gathering and analyzing data, measuring the baseline, and identifying gaps and solutions that can close those gaps. The Lean Six Sigma methodology lent itself very well to addressing this problem. However, since the company did not have the resources in-house and neither the intention to build the capability to drive the program, in this case it made sense for them to hire an external consultant with Lean Six Sigma expertise who came in and drove a structured project and was able to come up with the recommendations in three months.

Chapter 6

Establishing the Continuous Improvement Organization and Infrastructure

"Quality is not an accident. It is always the result of intelligent effort." – John Ruskin, English writer and critic 1819 -1900

In the previous chapter we looked at when it makes more sense to build an internal capability versus hiring an external consultant. As we now know, a sustainable continuous improvement program requires the right corporate infrastructure in place that can support and build the continuous improvement program.

But before we get to the details of how a typical organization that is required to build the internal capability would look like, let's briefly visit the support structure required for external consultants.

External Consultants:

External consultants are typically engaged by a sponsor of the continuous improvement initiative, and that is generally a big plus for the ultimate success of the program as the sponsors are mostly in a senior leadership position. However, it is not sufficient to just have a sponsor of the program–at a minimum different business leaders needs to be engaged in the effort as they are the stakeholders and, in most cases, process owners as well who will ultimately be impacted by and mostly benefit from the initiatives. In addition forming a committee that is responsible for overseeing the consultant's work not only gets the buy-in from the stakeholders but also makes it easier to get resources who can support the consultants with data and subject matter knowledge and ultimately make the initiatives successful. In many of the organizations we have seen, the consultants primarily come in as trainers to build the internal capability and the steering committee can actually identify key strategic initiatives as well as high performing individuals with the right skill set who can work on the critical initiatives. In other organizations where the consultant is engaged to drive real life projects, the steering committee can make sure the consultant engages the proper resources and is also delivering on the expectations from the project.

However, it is important to note that if there is no corporate wide initiative to implement a continuous improvement program and external consultants are leveraged for just imparting Lean or Six Sigma Green Belt or Black Belt training to individuals in one or two departments, a steering committee is not needed. In these kind of situations, where a group within an organization is "testing the waters," just having the departmental head as the sponsor or champion of the initiative is sufficient. In many cases this might actually be a great way to get started with Lean Six Sigma. The initial group becomes the pilot group, and their project success validates the fact that Lean Six Sigma can be applied and can generate great success across the entire organization.

Internal Program:

Successfully building an internal program requires a department staffed with fulltime, dedicated resources whose primary focus should be in building the continuous improvement program. Almost all the companies that are recognized globally as leaders in continuous improvement have a quality or continuous improvement department that is responsible for driving the program and delivering to the business as per commitments made. The actual work of program managing the continuous improvement initiative falls on a certified Lean Six Sigma Master Black Belt–companies who are just starting their continuous improvement program can actually benefit from hiring a skilled and experienced MBB from outside the company who has the experience in building these kinds of programs. As we have discussed elsewhere, a proven continuous improvement practitioner in the form of a certified Lean Six Sigma Master Black Belt (LSSMBB) can drive almost any continuous improvement program, irrespective of the continuous improvement methodology that is chosen. Another advantage with hiring a certified LSSMBB lies in the fact that Lean Six Sigma certification is probably the only industry accepted and globally recognized certification in the continuous improvement world and assures a minimum level of knowledge and understanding of the different continuous improvement methodologies. There are a few other certifications like QFD certification, Kaizen certification, BPM certification etc., and individuals having these kinds of certifications can also bring lot of value to a continuous improvement program. When it comes to developing internal training curriculum and infrastructure, the company can also leverage the LSSMBB instead of having to depend on external consultants and thereby save a significant amount of costs as well as be able to design a curriculum that fits in with the company's culture.

Opportunity for Growth:

As previously mentioned, a successful and visible internal quality or continuous improvement program can actually help in retaining talented staff as well as attract best candidates from the outside world. When such a program exists it becomes an attractive vehicle to reward high achievers grow within the business. In most companies with a successful and well recognized continuous improvement program that we have observed, high performing candidates with potential for future growth are selected to get trained as Green Belts. As part of their training, these candidates work on one or more projects in their respective area of work and gain a better understanding of how their department and more importantly processes within that department function. Once they have completed the Green Belt training and receive certification (after successful completion of a requisite number of projects), a select few with high leadership program are then sent by their management to go through the more rigorous Black Belt training. As part of Black Belt training, the successful candidates are expected to complete a cross functional project with significant benefits to the business. Working on these projects benefits the candidates in various ways–it develops them as leaders capable of delivering on major initiatives, it gives them visibility to senior leadership, and finally it is a great way for these individuals to learn more about other departments or overall business. Even though this sounds very logical on paper, in reality few companies have been really able to get this right for various reasons but most notably due to lack of top level support for the program.

Reward and Recognition Mechanism:

Reinforcement is probably the most important step in ensuring a successful change. As the saying goes, success breeds success. The next chapter addresses how and why the implementation of a successful continuous improvement program is very much dependent on proper change management. Also Appendix 1 analyzes 3M's failed Six Sigma program and hypothesizes how a proper change management methodology and implementation would have resulted in a potentially different ending. However, we have seen many companies that do not have a formal process in place to reward and recognize successful projects. On the other hand, most companies that have been successful in building a continuous improvement culture treat the initiatives and projects as mission critical with executive level visibility and support, and individuals vie to get the opportunity to work on these projects because of the potential for recognition and career growth.

Having the Right Sized Infrastructure:

Managing and running a successful continuous improvement program can be pretty difficult and companies who have shown commitment to the program have ensured that enough resources are dedicated to it. However, that does not mean that a company needs to hire a bunch of Master Black Belts. In fact, as the chart shows below, MBBs as a percentage of total employees should not be more than 0.1 percent. The areas where the company needs to invest more would be around program management, training, developing internal Green Belts, a few Black Belts, and in ensuring that successful projects are suitably recognized and rewarded.

Company	Number of Employees	MBBs	MBB as % of Employees
Starwood Hotels and Resorts, North America	150000	6	0.004%
McKesson Corp.	32160	18	0.056%
Pfizer Inc.	110000	36	0.033%
Merck & Co. Inc.	94000	80	0.085%
UnitedHealthcare Services	33000	6	0.018%
American Eurocopter Corp.	850	1	0.118%
Ecolab Inc.	26000	6	0.023%
Cardinal Health Inc.	32000	17	0.053%
TELUS Corp.	36000	5	0.014%
Computacenter AG & Co. oHG	3900	4	0.103%

Source: *iSixSigma Magazine*, March/Aril 2011

Case Study:

The United State Postal Service (USPS) has a Lean Six Sigma program in place to drive process improvements. Usually at USPS, Lean Six Sigma Black Belts are brought in as consultants or contractors for a longer term (around five years) reporting to an assigned manager and are responsible for identifying opportunities, reporting metrics, and training, in addition to driving process improvement projects.

Chapter 7

Change Management and Continuous Improvement

"Successful change, at its core is rooted in something much simpler: How to facilitate change with one person" – Jeffrey M. Hiatt

"Everyone thinks of changing the world but no one thinks of changing himself" – Leo Tolstoy

There is an interesting equation that process improvement practitioners like to quote all the time: Q x A = E

Simply speaking, it says that Effective Results is a function of Quality of Solution and Acceptance of Solution. What it really tells us is that effective results cannot be achieved by just the technical quality of the solution. In order to get effective results, there needs to be a sound cultural strategy as well as one that encourages the acceptance and embracing of the solution and that is what is called Change Management.

The importance of change management to successful continuous improvement initiatives cannot be impressed enough. The book *The Six Sigma Way* says that, "(e)mbarking on a Six Sigma initiative begins with a decision to change." And anytime there is a change it needs to be managed. Otherwise the transformation initiative is bound to fail. Studies have shown that more than 60 percent of transformational initiatives fail, not due to the lack of technical or resources, but rather due to the lack of proper change management.

Any leader who wants to drive a successful continuous improvement program should keep in mind that the soft stuff is the hard stuff. Just hiring a Black Belt or Lean Expert with the right credentials is not going to ensure the success of the initiative. As we have discussed in other chapters, we have always seen that continuous improvement programs have been successful only when there was visible senior leadership support and commitment to the program as well as a planned change management initiative tied to the program to ensure that all employees are moving from the current state to the expected future state with the program.

In fact, we have observed that putting a program management office in place to start with the program management in itself is a change management initiative. This becomes more important when an organization has an existing Enterprise PMO and a separate Enterprise Quality Organization that drives the program. Invariably the question comes up around ownership of these projects, after the initial few continuous improvement projects are successfully implemented. Turf wars are sure to happen unless a proper change management exercise is carried out at the beginning of the program deployment.

A very interesting article was published online recently titled "What Went Wrong with Six Sigma?" This is one of the few published materials that has tried to explain the failures of Six Sigma initiatives primarily because of poorly implemented change management. The authors state, "[w]hile very effective at controlling processes, it is those elements that are harder to control, such as employee behavior and innovation/ideation, which can hinder its long-term success." They also further write that most of the continuous improvement initiatives fail as success becomes a short-term phenomenon and cannot be sustained over a longer period of time. By taking a behavior-focused approach to change, the change becomes sustainable.

Behavior-focused change "helps the workers change the way they feel and think about their jobs by aligning attitudes and behaviors with the systems and process changes, as well with the overall direction of the company."

The reason change becomes sustainable with change management is because it answers the key question people ask every time they are faced with a change–what is in it for me and how is it going to impact my life or my job? There are a couple of well known change management models that can actually be tied in with any continuous improvement initiative to make it more successful.

The need for change management becomes even more important when a continuous improvement initiative is implemented in a services industry. In the services industry most of the process improvement root causes usually have a human element involved–like training issues, behavioral issues, etc. A company that does not follow proper change management procedures while implementing the continuous improvement program will not be able to get the benefits of the program once the projects are rolled out because of the resistance to change. Home Depot is a great example where the people on the front lines resisted the change. We are not going to get into the merits of whether Six Sigma methodology was even the right methodology for that company's culture, but even if it were, because of the resistance to change from the people who actually worked on the floors of the store, the program would have most likely failed. In an article in *Bloomberg Businessweek* that was published in January 2007, the then CEO, Bob Nardelli, was described as "autocratic and stubborn" by a store manager and his style was resented by the employees, and they were never motivated enough to support his Six Sigma initiative. Another telling comment in the same article mentioned that, "He seemed less concerned about people being friendly." Probably not the right change management for a team in the "orange big-box stores" who believed that customers came to Home Depot not because the products were necessarily cheaper, but rather because they can discuss and get advice from a real and hopefully friendly representative.

As per a Price Waterhouse Cooper study that was carried out a few years ago, 75 percent of all transformation initiatives fail or do not meet the intended goal[1]. In fact, more than half of the failures are attributable to poor change management related to people issues, communication issues, and the culture of the organization.

Change Management Models:

Let us take a look at three most commonly applied change models in the industry

1. ADKAR®

2. Kotter 8 Step Change Model

3. William Bridges Three Step Transition Model

ADKAR®	Kotter Model	Bridges Model
• Awareness	• Create Urgency	• Ending, Losing, Letting Go
• Desire	• Form a Powerful Coalition	• The Neutral Zone
• Knowledge	• Create a Vision for Change	• The New Beginning
• Ability	• Communicate the Vision	
• Reinforcement	• Remove obstacles	
	• Create Short-Term Wins	

	• Build on the Change • Anchor the Changes in the Company Culture	

ADKAR®:

The ADKAR® change management framework is based on the basic premise that change management needs to happen at an individual level. This was created by Jeffrey Hiatt of Prosci Research. ADKAR® is an acronym for Awareness, Desire, Knowledge, Ability, and Reinforcement

- Awareness – Awareness is the first step towards enabling successful change. This awareness helps address questions around why the change is being made now and what will happen if the change is not made. This creates a strong reason behind why the change is needed and gives an individual who is required to change a process or direction, the answer to "what is in it for me." The acceptance of awareness message is influenced by the person's understanding of the current state, the person's individual cognitive style, and their perception of the need for change and problem solution style, the credibility of the person sending the change message, and the presence of misinformation or rumors that might blank out the change message. The awareness of need for change is easier to create in the presence of external drivers.

- Desire – Desire represents the motivation and commitment to accepting and participating in a change and depends on the individual's choices. There are several factors that influence this decision and motivation, like the nature of the change, how the individual perceives the organization and surrounding situation, and the individual's current personal situation and motivating factors.

- Knowledge – Knowledge represents how the change will be implemented and includes training and education on skill set required for training, knowledge of how to use any new process or tools, and understanding of the changed roles and responsibilities. There are a few factors in interplay that ultimately determine the extent to which an individual can acquire the necessary knowledge required for a change.

- Ability – Ability represents the capability of an individual to implement the change. Psychological blocks, physical abilities, intellectual capability, time available to develop the needed skills, and the availability of resources to support the individual during a change are the different elements that can impact the ability of an individual to respond to and accept a change.

- Reinforcement – Reinforcement is the final step in a change process that ensures the change is sustained, builds the momentum during the change, and also helps in ensuring a successful change initiative that becomes a part of an organization's past history once completed.

  Note that the process steps are sequential in nature and one needs to happen before the other can happen. For example, there cannot be a desire to support a change unless there is the awareness around the need for change.

Let's now do a very simplified analysis of a Lean Six Sigma program implementation as a change management initiative using ADKAR®. The first step is the *awareness* for change. Unless business leaders realize the benefits of Six Sigma and why the company or division needs to adopt the methodology, the program is never even going to get started. And even if there is the awareness about the need to implement a Six Sigma program, the next step is the *desire* to go ahead and introduce the program–past experience with Six Sigma can both impact the desire as well as knowledge steps. Next comes *knowledge* and this is where the business leader's understanding and expectation of the methodology plays a big role. Once these three are in place, then the leader can start assessing the *ability* of the individuals within the team and making hiring decisions as needed. Finally to make this methodology stick, the leader will have to *reinforce* the change.

Kotter 8 Step Change Model:

The Kotter Model is probably the most used change management model in the last decade. Even companies like GE adopted the Kotter model as part of their Six Sigma change management curriculum. This model was developed by John Kotter, a professor at Harvard Business School and author of multiple bestselling books on management. According to Kotter, change management needs to follow an eight step process:

- Establishing a Sense of Urgency – Business leaders need to eliminate a sense of complacency or minimize the impact. However, this is not as easy as it sounds. Most company cultures reward cautious managers, and it is very difficult for them to increase urgency levels all at once. Kotter suggests a few ways to raise the urgency level: by creating a crisis, eliminating obvious examples of excess, setting stretch and/or unattainable performance goals, and so forth.

- Creating the Guiding Coalition – Kotter states that it is impossible for one individual, however powerful he or she is, to develop the right vision and communicate it to large number of people, remove obstacles, create quick wins, and be able to lead and manage changes across the entire organization. Building a strong guiding coalition is essential to any organizational changes.

- Developing a Vision and Strategy – Kotter defines vision as a picture of the future and explains why that future needs to be created. An effective vision clarifies the direction of change and why it is required.

- Communicating the Change Vision – Any transformational activity achieves its full potential when everybody within an organization has a common understanding of the goals and direction. However, in reality managers usually under communicate. Having a simple message reduces the time and effort required towards effective communication.

- Empowering Employees for Broad Based Action – This step includes removing structural barriers and providing employees with the needed training. Leaders need to ensure there is incentive for employees to make the change. At the same time, any issues with supervisors' resistance to change needs to be promptly addressed as well.

- Generating Short-term Wins – Major changes usually take a lot of time. However, except for the zealous believers, most everybody expects to see the evidence the change is delivering the result. In our experience we have found that this had almost always made the difference between a successful and failed continuous improvement initiative. Instead of depending on sheer luck to get some wins, leadership actually needs to plan for creating short-term wins.

- Consolidating Gains and Producing More Change
  – Business leaders must not start celebrating too
  early. If they let up before the job is done, critical
  momentum is lost and the change may actually
  regress.

- Anchoring New Approaches in the Culture – When
  initiatives are led by senior business leaders and
  the transformation program was ever visible any
  cultural influence that might be incompatible with
  the changes gets overwhelmed. However, as soon
  as the focus gets shifted, the culture starts to
  reassert itself. It is important to note that cultural
  change comes last, not first in the transformation
  process.

William Bridges' Three Phase Transition Model:

This is another popular change management model that was proposed by William Bridges. William Bridges is considered a leader in transition and change management and was rated by *The Wall Street Journal* in 1993 as one of the ten most popular executive development consultants in the United States. The three steps of William Bridges' transition model are:

Ending, Losing, and Letting Go – In this phase individuals have to let go of the old identity as well as their way of doing work. This is an ending phase and business leaders need to support their people as they deal with the losses. The fact that no one thinks about endings or draws up plans to manage their impact on people is identified as the single biggest reason behind failure of organizational change efforts. As per Bridges "the first task of change management is to understand the desired outcome and how to get there, the first task of transition management is to convince people to leave home."

The Neutral Zone – The neutral zone is the in-between phase when the old is gone but the new state has not yet been fully operationalized. This is the phase where "critical psychological realignments and repatternings take place." To be successful in driving the change, leadership needs to ensure that this zone is viewed as an opportunity to create something new and exciting. If handled properly, people emerge from this zone more comfortable and confident about the new change.

The New Beginning – As per Bridges the beginning will take place only after the people experiencing the change have come through the wilderness and are ready to make the emotional commitment to do things the new way and see themselves as new people. Leadership needs to communicate the purpose of the new beginning very clearly.

We will now look at the same example of Lean Six Sigma implementation and see how William Bridges' model can be applied to ensure successful adoption of the program. In the "Ending, Letting Go" phase, both leadership and employees need to realize why they will have to let go of the old way of doing things and will now have to move to a more structured, data driven, and analysis based approach to process improvements. In the neutral zone, the leadership will launch the program, start doing in-house training for Belts (or hire external consultants) and identify projects. The success or failure of the implementation program will depend on how well people are led through this phase. If the change is managed properly, in the final stage (new beginning) all the people in the organization will have a clear understanding of why the company chose Lean Six Sigma as the continuous improvement methodology and will have full emotional commitment to the success of the program.

We have found that any of the above change models work equally well, though the advantage with ADKAR® is that it includes assessment tools as well as templates for developing various change plans. Ultimately the business leader will have to decide which model to apply for the success of the improvement initiative.

In some rare cases we have come across improvement initiatives that have evolved from the grassroots without real leadership support or vision. At times behavioral change can be driven by the project leader as well even though the overall continuous improvement initiative support might not be there initially from the senior leadership. We will look into this further later on in this book regarding what the project leader or Belt can do to drive acceptance by leadership in such instances. However, we would like to point out that unless senior leadership support and sponsorship is obtained, ultimately any structured continuous improvement methodology is not going to stick in an organization. We believe that implementing a continuous improvement project requires structured change management, and as per a 2009 study conducted by Prosci research, the greatest contributor to any change initiative is "Active and visible executive sponsorship."

Case Study:

Home Depot had launched it Six Sigma program in 2001, but by 2007 stock prices dropped by around 8 percent when former CEO Robert Nardelli resigned. The company also dropped from the top spot on the American Customer Satisfaction Index rankings among major retailers to the bottom in 2005. The ouster of Robert Nardelli was seen by many as proof that the Six Sigma methodology does not work in improving either the top line or bottom line for a company. However, 60 percent of all Six Sigma initiatives fail because of poor change management, according to a renowned Six Sigma author and consultant who has been involved with Six Sigma since the early 1980s.

An article that appeared in the *destinationCRM* webzine titled "Six Sigma: What went wrong?" very succinctly summed up the reason behind the failure as, "At Six Sigma locations, a sizable gap may exist: While it might be clear what type of change is needed to technically enhance throughput, the success of that effort hinges on whether that behavior is modified permanently. Process improvements may perfectly achieve their objectives, but the workforce may not be prepared to accept them as part of their daily routines." It is this lack of initial acceptance of the program that probably produced results that were sub-optimal compared to the expectations and led to the former CEOs ouster.

It is very important to mention though that the Six Sigma program at Home Depot did not die with the exit of Bob Nardelli. A quick search of the Home Depot Career link in November 2011, gave thirty-seven posted positions that required some level of Six Sigma knowledge!

Note: ADKAR® is a registered trademark of Prosci

Chapter 8

Why Continuous Improvement Programs Fail

"If you only have a hammer you tend to see every problem as a nail." – Abraham Maslow, Psychologist

"Success is not final, failure is not fatal: it is the courage to continue that counts." – Winston Churchill

An astute continuous improvement leader in a global company that was struggling with customer churn and falling market share figured out that if the people kept doing things the way they had been in the past, the company would not be able to stymie the loss in market share or customer satisfaction. She rightly went ahead, built a high level business case and got the approval to hire a Lean Six Sigma Black Belt with stellar credentials. There was a specific project that was identified as the most critical one and the Black Belt hit the ground running. The Black Belt quickly assembled a team and within a few months was able to achieve huge improvements. This pilot project was immediately embraced by senior leadership and became *the* project everyone talked about. The improvement leader was given the go-ahead to hire more resources and establish a formal Lean Six Sigma program. The normal ending to this story would be "and they lived happily ever after" or rather "drove continuous improvement happily ever after." But unfortunately it did not happen that way. Soon after the initial euphoria died down and a few Green Belts were trained the projects started to get delayed. This in turn led senior leadership to quickly interpret the Lean Six Sigma methodology was not going to give the breakthrough results as was earlier expected. The continuous improvement leader and the Black Belt were left spending more time trying to explain why the projects were not moving on and delivering on the promised outcomes instead of working on the projects.

Unfortunately this is a common scenario with many Six Sigma and Lean deployments. In our experience, the failure rate of Lean and Six Sigma initiatives, which includes incomplete projects is extremely high. This is also supported by information available in the public domain. In various articles that are available in the public domain, the failure estimate for Lean initiatives ranges between 40 to 55 percent. Likewise the estimated failure rate for Six Sigma projects ranges from 37 percent to as high as 60 percent! But we have been able to build successful continuous improvement programs in different organizations (and industries) and truly believe that this can be avoided. Let us now look at the key factors that decide the success or failure of a continuous improvement endeavor in an organization.

Leadership Support:

If there is one factor that can make or break a successful continuous improvement program, it is top level leadership support. In an article titled "Lean Manufacturing's Next Life" that was published in ChiefExecutive.Net, the CEO of a sixty-year-old family owned company, WIKA Alexander Wiegand SE that has significantly reduced manufacturing lead times using Lean states, "I still participate one or two times a year in a Kaizen workshop. Everybody in the company knows that I am always very interested in the results and seeing what has changed."

In the previous chapter we briefly touched upon how continuous improvement can be driven without top leadership support initially. However, in order to sustain the continuous improvement program, top leadership buy in is extremely important. There are numerous examples of companies that have started a program with mid-level management support that ultimately fizzled out within a couple of years. At the same time all the major success stories that we hear are for companies that have had strong top level leadership support and commitment. Leadership support also helps create a strong sense of urgency and in setting up appropriate expectations. The first step, and probably the most important, is to set the right tone for your continuous improvement (CI) journey. The reason and need for change needs to be clear, concise, and well understood at all levels of the organization, from the lowest level (you might want to choose another word instead of "lowest") of employees to the executive leadership. The leadership needs to set the expectations for the entire company. Many organizations start CI programs as a flavor of the month, but without clear strategy behind it the program dies down without reaching its full potential.

Also, as we discussed in another chapter many business leaders support and deploy Six Sigma or Lean programs with the sole intention of driving hard cost reductions. But the reality is that all continuous improvement initiatives do not have cost savings or revenue gain that are hard dollar numbers, and this is probably not the right expectation for business leaders to have from any continuous improvement initiative.

However, initial leadership resistance to change management can be removed by generating the proof of concept early on and getting buy in from the leaders. The following section has been adapted from the article published on iSixSigma's website in June 2011 under the heading "Driving Six Sigma Success without Top-Level Support" that was written by one of this book's authors.

This kind of situation usually arises when a departmental leader initiates a Six Sigma or Lean program without real support from leadership. Once a few projects get completed, usually leaders buy-in and commit additional resources to the program and it starts growing. In these scenarios, there are four critical factors that can ensure success of the program in the long run:

Factor 1: The project leader needs to show proof of concept and ensure a successful project with quick turnaround.

Factor 2: The project leader needs to build a team made up of individuals who need the victory. The project should directly address the team's pain points with a process.

Factor 3: The project leader needs to demystify Lean or Six Sigma and avoid using jargons. In the initial stages it is easier to get buy-in by avoiding technical Six Sigma language

Factor 4: The project leader needs to be his or her own champion and key cheerleader of the project. Once the project is successful, the project leader needs to take the initiative to advertise and sell the benefits within the company and even outside.

To summarize, even without top level support a Six Sigma or Lean program can be successfully established and eventually sustained in an organization. However, in order to achieve that it is important to select the right project, have the right team, stay away from technical jargon and acronyms initially, and communicate project success once the first project is successfully completed. Chevron is a great example where a grassroots program started by a few zealous employees in one division ultimately became a corporate wide initiative saving the company millions of dollars since 2008. We will cover the Chevron example in greater details in the Case Study section at the end of this chapter

```
                    ┌─────────────────┐
                    │ 1. Show proof of│
                    │    Concept      │
                    └─────────────────┘
                            ⬆
┌──────────────┐                          ┌──────────────┐
│4. Be your own│◄── Successful Six Sigma Program ──►│2. Create a  │
│  Cheerleader │                          │ winning Team │
└──────────────┘                          └──────────────┘
                            ⬇
                    ┌─────────────────┐
                    │ 3. Demystify Six│
                    │    Sigma        │
                    └─────────────────┘
```

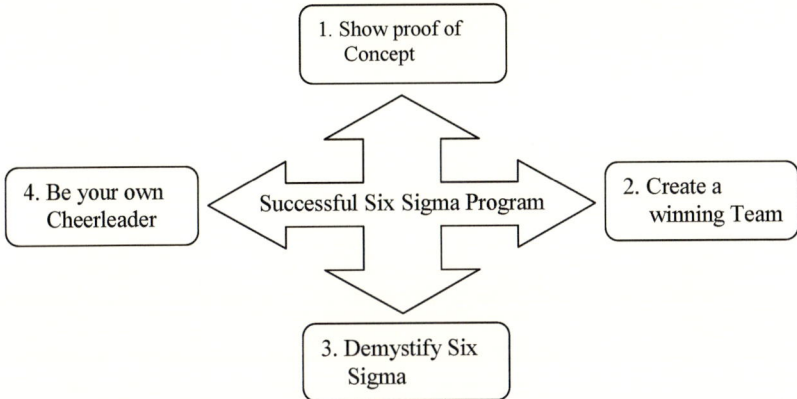

Company Not Ready:

Most of the Six Sigma or Lean programs that have failed can be attributed to the fact that the company was not ready to implement. As discussed in a previous chapter, both Six Sigma and Lean requires that the right continuous improvement infrastructure is put in place before the program is launched. Any continuous improvement initiative is going to fail if the company is not devoting enough resources to the initiative in general and projects in particular. Numerous companies have launched Six Sigma or Lean programs that stumbled and suffered just because the Belts or Lean leaders did not have the time to continue working on their projects after they spent time going through rigorous training. Or in those cases where a project gets started the Belts face tremendous obstacles in getting team members and subject matter experts' participation. This leads to frustration for both the Belts or Lean leaders who struggle to meet their individual targets and the business leaders who were expecting great things from the program. In such scenarios it is better to wait to get both resources and commitment from the sponsor/champion as well as subject matter experts before launching the initiative. In addition the particular program, be it Six Sigma or Lean, requires the blessing of senior leaders. If top business leaders view Six Sigma or Lean as a fad of the month and don't see the strategic value these programs bring, then it might be worthwhile to show them the value of these methodologies and get them onboard before implementing a full-fledged program. As we have discussed in the previous section, if leadership is ambivalent to these programs and where the need is to get strong commitment, it might be possible to get their support by driving a pilot project to completion that generates breakthrough results.

Another factor to keep in mind is that Six Sigma is costly to implement and small companies might not have the capability to hire the right resources to make the program effective and hence struggle. As we discussed in Chapter 6, putting together the infrastructure and resources that can support a successful Lean or more importantly Six Sigma program takes considerable effort, money, and time. One solution for these companies would be to get the help of reliable Six Sigma experts and external consultants for targeted process improvement initiatives with a percent of revenue or cost reduction as the fees for the external consultants. This will be a better option for these small companies instead of trying to set up in-house capability.

And finally there needs to be an alignment of Lean Six Sigma implementation with the strategic business plan and direction. In order to achieve successful Lean Six Sigma implementation, there should be a clear link between improvement initiatives and the overall strategic plan for the organization. Some good examples of long term strategic goals are: to grow market shares by 25 percent in five years; to grow overall revenue by 50 percent in five years, etc. The continuous improvement initiatives should then be linked to this overall strategy: in other words, most of the Lean Six Sigma initiatives should link to how they will help the organization achieve its long-term strategic goals. One of the most common failure modes we see is that the CI function is on its own island. The root cause for this failure is typically a lack of linkage between business needs and continuous improvement initiatives. One real life example would be the continuous improvement group working on solely improving the 5S, while the factory's on time performance is past-due and heading in the wrong direction.

5S is a five phase Japanese workplace organization methodology. 5S denotes the five words that describes how to organize the workspace to get the maximum efficiency and effectiveness from a process. These are Sorting (keep things clean and organized like manufacturing tools, soft files etc.), Straightening (organize, identify and arrange everything e.g. file folders in hard drive, tools in tool box), Sweeping or Shining (ensure regular maintenance and cleaning), Standardizing (standardized process steps) and Sustaining (maintain and review standards). Even though it was initially developed in the manufacturing world, it has recently got widespread acceptance in transactional processes in the service industry as well. While 5S is extremely important and is the foundation for continuous improvement, the priorities should be balanced to support the business needs and to develop the CI culture that is required. If the balance is shifted towards the implementation of principles without direct link to business results, you are heading for trouble. In many cases, this shift in balance is what makes the senior leadership back out of their commitment to continuous improvement.

In order for continuous improvement to stick, the improvement must be meaningful to the business and to the leadership. Lean Six Sigma is simply a set of tools that helps organizations get the desired business results while creating a high performing workforce and outstanding employee satisfaction.

Copying Other Companies:

This may sound very basic, but many companies try to fit the GE model or the Motorola model or the Bank of America model to their Six Sigma program. Unfortunately this does not always work, since each company would have its unique culture, corporate strategy, and direction. The book *The Six Sigma Way* pointed this out way back in 2000 when it was first published. As the book says, "Following a fixed prescription, or modeling your effort after another company is guaranteed to fail–or come close." However, many organizations in the last decade chose to build Six Sigma programs modeled exactly after other organization's programs where Six Sigma was successfully deployed by hiring ex-MBBs or Black Belts from those organizations only to find out after a year or so that the program cannot be sustained within the new company.

One Approach Fits All:

Numerous business leaders have spoken up against using Six Sigma in innovation. This is a classic case of one size does not fit all. Six Sigma should be used where the process is structured and the company is trying to make the process more efficient and effective. Unfortunately, creativity and innovation does not follow a set or defined process and companies that have applied a *rigid* Six Sigma approach to the innovation process have undoubtedly suffered (readers should note the emphasis on the word rigid). 3M corporation which was renowned for its innovations a decade ago is an apt case in point where, after years of applying Six Sigma across all functions and measurably reducing innovation–which was the core competency of the company, it was finally dropped as a continuous improvement tool in R&D in 2007. As a corporation, 3M dropped from the *Bloomberg Businessweek* 2010 list of The 50 Most Innovative Companies Globally for the first time since 2004 when it was ranked number one. When James McNerney was hired as the CEO of 3M in 2000 from GE, he brought the Six Sigma concepts that were popularized by Jack Welch. The Six Sigma methodology, in fact, did help 3M in improving their processes and profits. As a June 2007 *Businessweek* article states, "The Six Sigma drive undoubtedly contributed to 3M's astronomical profitability improvements under McNerney; operating margins went from 17% in 2001 to 23% in 2005." However, the company found out that creativity was getting stifled when applied to the innovation process. George Buckley, the CEO who took over in 2007 said, "Invention is by its very nature a disorderly process" where a structured framework like DMAIC or DFSS will not be best suited. As of 2011, Six Sigma is still a preferred continuous improvement methodology at 3M but primarily in the supply chain and manufacturing areas. Note: even though Six Sigma was discontinued in the R&D division in 2007 at 3M, the company has not been able to make it back into the list of most innovative companies. So, the problem that 3M is facing in coming out with innovative products might be symptomatic of other issues within the company and not necessarily because of the deployment of Six Sigma across 3M. As we have seen in the case study in Chapter 1, Six Sigma has been successfully applied by Starwood hotels to come up with innovative services.

In a creativity conference sponsored by the Harvard Business School, Mark Fisherman, MD, president of the Novartis Institutes for Biomedical Research stated that, "If there is one device that has destroyed more innovation than any other, it is Six Sigma." Having said that, as leading neuropsychologist Madeleine Van Hecke et al. who have studied the effect of Six Sigma methodology on innovation said in *The Brain Advantage*, "The point is not to say that Six Sigma isn't valuable–just that there are times and places to apply it." A good example of where Six Sigma can be applied over the lifecycle of an innovative invention would be the new product introduction or new product development process. Once the creative thinkers and innovators have come up with a potential product, the design for Six Sigma methodology can absolutely be applied to develop a product that is free of defects, is launched on-time and within budget, and meets the customers' requirements. Another approach would be to apply tools like Quality Function Deployment, which is widely used in DMADV projects, to map current capabilities with customer needs and identify products for the future. Furthermore, Lean methodology and concepts of Kanban and Value Stream Mapping can be applied to reduce waste and inventory in the process, engage suppliers and distributors, and ensure lower costs in product development and distribution which in turn lead to higher margins for the business. In the article "Is Six Sigma Hard Sell Now?" that appeared in the *Chief*

Executive.net, Mike Nichols, president of the American Society for Quality was quoted as saying that, "Six Sigma as well as Lean and Process Management can help any organization execute better, and meet and exceed customer's expectations." He also believes that "the better a company becomes at executing, the more opportunities it opens up for innovations."

A much better example of the wrong application of Lean would be when a company is downsizing and reducing its workforce. Even though many leaders still do so, Lean should not be used as a tool to reduce workforce. As an eZine article states, "When a company needs a transformation, or specifically headcount reduction, this should be done prior to any continuous improvement initiative. [I]t is critical for Lean's success to educate the executives to the problems with headcount reduction. [P]eople will not find a way to eliminate their job [using Lean techniques]." Such kinds of initiatives are almost always set up to fail.

Poor Change Management:

We have already looked at the importance of change management to successful continuous improvement programs in the previous chapter. Any successful continuous improvement initiative needs significant change management. The reason Lean was so successful at Toyota was because of the commitment of the executive leadership to implement a company-wide quality initiative. Likewise, GE's success with Six Sigma is also because of Jack Welch's visible commitment to the methodology. It is almost impossible to change a company's culture and get people to adapt to a Six Sigma or Lean methodology and get projects completed successfully without managing change. The other reason this has become so important is because of some of the press around Six Sigma and Lean that touts these initiatives as tools for reducing workforce and cutting costs. This makes it even more difficult to get the support and participation from the people who do the actual work and drive process improvements. However, there are many companies out there with a somewhat functional continuous improvement program without real focus on managing change that needs to go hand-in-hand with both the program as well as individual continuous improvement projects. This usually leads to sub-optimal results and these companies never see the full benefit of a Six Sigma or Lean program. In extreme cases, a company might not even be ready to embrace a continuous improvement program and the lack of a proper assessment of change readiness will lead to failure of the initiative even before it is deployed. Appendix 2 discusses how change assessment can be carried out using the ADKAR® model that we reviewed in a previous chapter.

Reward and recognition mechanisms are also key change management attributes, and yet many companies that have a formal continuous improvement program in place do not have any formal reward and recognition program in place.

Improper Selection of Projects, Forcing Tools to Solve the Problem:

Most readers would be familiar with Abraham Maslow's famous quote around treating every problem as a nail when the only tool available is a hammer. Sadly this analogy holds true for many companies where continuous improvement initiatives have failed to take off. We have seen companies that launch a Six Sigma or Lean program with senior leadership's support but cannot show results because they are forcing all business problems to be tackled using the selected methodology. These companies end up spending valuable time and resources in training and building the capability but fail to execute on the projects. And the root cause for the failure is simple–those projects were just not suited to the methodology selected. We have already discussed elsewhere in this book how to select the right methodology that can help optimize the results from a project.

Change in Leadership Direction:

Businesses, at times need to change direction and continuous improvement initiatives in those times may take a back seat. This is commonly seen when a company is going through a crisis. A very common example is falling market share associated with decrease in revenue and net income. This gets exacerbated during recessionary periods and usually necessitates significant workforce reduction, and in such scenarios the continuous improvement program usually takes the hit as it is not considered mission critical to running the business in those times. Of course the root cause of the company going through this phase needs to be explored in the first place. A Lean organization usually does not have to go through massive layoff phases if they are doing their job right.

Sometimes leadership changes, and they bring in their own preferred methodology just because they have been exposed to it previously. This usually works but can become a pitfall if it is applied without really following a strategic approach to selecting the methodology. As mentioned earlier, 3M and Home Depot are great examples of this. In addition, leadership needs to understand that structured continuous improvement initiatives never give immediate results, and there is an upfront cost. In the *Hoshin Handbook* Pete Babich mentions that it takes at least three years for the Hoshin process to work properly. However, many leaders who are initially enthusiastic, subsequently lose patience once they feel the methodology is taking too long and either pull the plug or let it die a slow death by not visibly supporting it.

Change in Business Situation:

Likewise, when a company gets taken over the continuous improvement program gets affected. Many times during those transition phases the focus shifts from long term strategic continuous improvement to getting short term gains. Usually that leads to a shift from Six Sigma to Lean.

Lack of Reporting/Business Analytics Capability:

Setup a strong reporting capability that will enable you to link the Lean or Six Sigma results to the bottom-line. Even though cost saving is not the entire reason for implementation of Lean Six Sigma, it is extremely important to be able to link the improvements to the bottom-line or to the long-term strategic goals. If the strategic alignment was properly carried out, then this step will be easier to apply. At the end of the day, most of the Lean Six Sigma improvements should correlate to the bottom-line and/or how it helps the organization to reach its strategic plans and objectives. Also, this will help to ensure that the finance team is on board with the planned improvements and their expected benefits. The finance team should be part of the planning phase of the Lean Six Sigma implementation so that the estimated savings/benefits are calculated well before the implementation.

Seven Steps towards building an effective CI initiative

And lastly, here is the final set of steps that needs to be put in place in order to have a truly performing CI initiative in an organization:

1. Selecting the right people to run your LSS program: This step will truly make or break your LSS journey. As we all know, truly talented people suited for Lean Six Sigma are hard to find. Our experience shows that it is best to develop your own internal talent rather than hiring from outside. However, when you are just getting started, you need outside talent to get the journey going. If you are new and just getting started, you should select an internal leader who understands the business and the LSS culture the best to lead the initiative. Often, when you hire someone from outside to lead this initiative when it is new, it takes time for the individual to understand the operations, business, and the company culture. It is much easier to train someone internally who understands the operations, business, and culture of Lean Six Sigma, than to familiarize outside talent with your company's culture. Also, companies need to be careful about hiring Lean

Six Sigma professionals who are inflexible and unwilling to modify their approach to suit the business and cultural needs. The Lean Six Sigma concepts are straightforward, but the application of these concepts is never due to the nature of the business and the culture of the company. Hence, you need to select the people who are capable of quickly diagnosing and understanding the business nature, the existing culture, and developing an approach that is best suited for your organization.

2.   Selecting a right outside company to help you: Almost all companies need support from an outside service provider to get them started in the right direction. Companies should look for someone who is willing to partner with them to implement the principles in a way that will work with the culture of that organization. While the concepts of Lean Six Sigma are straightforward, their application to each company can be as unique and diverse as the company itself. Often an outside company will help you ensure that your organization is protected from the pitfalls of Lean Six Sigma implementation. Ideally, you will need to find a partner who has lived this role and has experienced it first hand, not just consulted!

3.   Training the leadership first: If there is one initiative that will truly test leadership, this is it. Lean Six Sigma will test your leadership skills, support, know-how, and relentless follow-up and follow through skills. It is not uncommon for people to say our continuous improvement efforts failed due to lack of leadership support and commitment. We challenge this by asserting that the real root of the cause is that the leadership typically do not have the knowledge that is required to support these initiatives. In many cases, they truly do not know what to do or how

to manage the Lean Six Sigma world. This lack of knowledge is, more often than not, one of the single most cited reasons these initiatives fail. We strongly recommend starting your LSS implementations with leadership training first. After all, it is only fair to train them before you expect them to support it.

4. Creating quick wins to excite the organization: In order for LSS implementation to strive and be successful, at the beginning of the Lean Six Sigma journey, an organization *must* create quick wins. Often, companies pick the easiest thing to fix to demonstrate the concepts which may or may not have significant impact to the business. To avoid this failure mode, we recommend that companies go for the biggest impact project first. In addition to helping the business solve one of its most complex problems, this creates the excitement in the company atmosphere that is required to be successful. To further spread this excitement throughout the organization, some of the most popular ways to communicate successes are company-wide newsletters and webcast sharing. Creating and communicating success are areas where your outside consulting company will be of great help in identifying the right project and successfully achieving results to excite the whole organization.

5. Expanding it Enterprise-wide: Now that you have the right people, the right leadership and the whole organization excited about Lean Six Sigma, it is time to expand the concepts enterprise-wide. Most organizations typically start in one of their departments or functions in their company. Organizations should move quickly to expand the application of the concepts throughout the company before it is attached only to the function

where it is started, e.g., "It is a shop floor thing. It doesn't apply to the offices." Also, in order to achieve the fullest potential of Lean Six Sigma, the applications of these principles should be extended to suppliers and customers of the organization. The timing of integrating suppliers and customers will vary depending on the industry and maturity level of the organizations.

6.   Leveraging the improvements to GROW the business: This is one of the single most important reasons why Lean Six Sigma dies down after a successful start. Also, this is *the* biggest missed opportunity after all the hard work has been put in to ensure the successful beginnings of Lean Six Sigma. Many organizations fail to leverage their LSS success to win more business from their existing clients or acquire new clients/businesses. The most common reason any company wants to start their Lean Six Sigma journey is to grow market share and profitability. One of the easiest ways to improve your profitability is to increase your net sales with relatively same level of staffing. Lean Six Sigma, if it is done correctly, will help you to achieve this.

7.   Pay-for-Performance for All: The last piece of this puzzle can be explained perfectly with the adage "Put your money where your mouth is." All of the successful organizations in CI have a pay-for-performance program for all employees. While many organizations have bonus programs for certain levels of employees, it does not typically excite the entire organization. In many cases, it only sends the wrong message to the employees who are not in the bonus program– Why should I work hard when it is other employees who get more money? No matter how much we don't want to believe it, *behavior*

follows money. Though the level of reward will be/should be different, all employees should be rewarded for exceptional performance in addition to their regular salary. What we have seen is that the companies that have these programs have a great sense of ownership and accountability at all levels of the organization, and every employee is a leader and able to call out poor performance when they see it.

Case Study:

In 2000 a small group of Chevron employees launched a business unit deployment of Six Sigma. In fact, the first project was carried out by just six employees in 1998 and 1999. However, even though the project resulted in reduction in operating costs by about 30 percent at the Chevron Lost Hills water treatment plant, no one really paid attention since there was no leadership support or commitment to the program. However, one individual who was aware of the fantastic results achieved by the Lost Hills team started a formal program in Indonesia with a training program. Even then it was a "hope for the best" kind of situation with no leadership support behind Six Sigma as a formally recognized methodology. The good thing was that leadership did support the team to go ahead and do it and just informed the leadership team when the projects were done.

In 2001 the results started coming in from the first set of projects launched in Indonesia and leadership finally gave the permission to run a Six Sigma training program. An interesting side note: Chevron has since then outsourced all their training needs to external consultants even though they have qualified trainers and resources in house. This is because Chevron believes the resources should be focused on running Lean Six Sigma projects instead of spending time delivering training. Subsequently senior leadership agreed to support a deployment at the San Joaquin Valley (SJV) operations. This was Chevron's first top-down business unit deployment of Six Sigma in 2001.

The success of the SJV deployment caught attention and soon other units starting deploying Six Sigma as well. Currently Chevron is well on its way to having formal Lean Six Sigma in place for all global upstream business units.

This is an excellent example where a continuous improvement methodology took hold in a giant global organization without top level support or sponsorship in the initial stages. We believe that a few factors worked in the program's favor. First, even though leadership were not committed or visibly supporting initially, they were not against the methodology and, in fact, tolerated it. This is a huge factor. As we have mentioned earlier if leadership is dead against a methodology then there is no chance of it getting accepted. Secondly, the initial few projects were able to show significant business benefits which got the attention of leadership. And finally had the formal deployment at SJV failed, the program would not have taken off in the manner it did.

Chapter 9

Measurement and Tracking of Continuous Improvement Programs

"You can't manage what you can't measure" – *Anonymous*

"There are so many men who can figure costs, and so few who can measure values." - *Author Unknown*

In many organizations, we have seen continuous improvement efforts being led by a middle level business leader who is usually managing the quality organization. The real challenge with this structure is that the tracking, reporting, and visibility to the initiative in general and projects in particular do not always reach up to executive leadership level. And this causes quite a few issues–first of all executive leadership is focused on costs and do not see the value of projects that might not have a hard dollar impact, for example projects that lead to reducing workload or increasing customer satisfaction. There are only a few companies we have come across that have reached a level of maturity where they can link and demonstrate exact contribution of a project to the increase in customer satisfaction scores and also quantify the dollar value of each percentage gain in customer satisfaction to the company. Many times the continuous improvement organizations have to face pressure to reduce headcounts because of the perception that the program is not delivering. And this is where it becomes extremely important to ensure that proper measurement and reporting processes are in place around the continuous improvement program and the results are shared with top level executive leadership.

Lack of Management By Objectives or Performance Measures for Green Belts:

Many Six Sigma projects, especially Green Belt projects fail because of the lack of accountability on projects they are driving. Green Belts usually work on projects in their own area and if they are not held formally accountable or responsible for the completion of the Six Sigma projects, chances are that the projects will take a secondary priority to managing day to day activity around the processes they own at the same time. With the lack of proper metrics and reporting systems in place, these projects never get the right visibility and are not tracked by leadership which decreases the motivation of the Belts. Based on our experience, this can be extremely fatal for a newly launched process improvement initiative. One way to mitigate this would be to link successful completion of the Six Sigma project to the Green Belts' annual performance measures.

Applying Structured Process to Link and Measure Project Progress Tied to Critical Business Goals:

Hoshin Kanri, or any such approach including Balanced Score Card or Management By Objectives, to tie projects to overall strategy will ensure success of the initiatives as results tie directly to CEO's goals. Hoshin Kanri is a strategic planning and strategic management methodology that we covered in the first chapter. The implementation of the continuous improvement initiative can be treated as an element of the Hoshin Plan and progress reviewed regularly as per the Plan-Do-Check-Act cycle.

What it does is that it helps align continuous improvement initiatives to overall business strategy and, in effect, becomes a powerful change management tool. It also effectively ties each project to an owner who is responsible for meeting the targets and delivering on the projects.

Let us now look at the approach that can be followed to develop the continual improvement measurement system that caters to the need of the different stakeholders.

Step 1: Identify Business Goals and Objectives. For middle level managers who are starting a program it will be important to reach out to senior level leadership to understand the business' key priorities and goals.

Step 2: Ensure that the selected projects can be linked to the objectives and goals.

Step 3: Establish metrics and goals for the continuous improvement project that are linked directly to the overall business goals. This will be very crucial to demonstrate the linkage between the continuous improvement program and improvement in business goals in future.

Step 4: Develop a measurement system capable of reporting the metrics chosen for the projects. In our experience having access to a database analysts plays a big role in not only implementing the proper measurement system but also making sure that the metrics (and associated drivers) can be reported with confidence on a periodic basis. This is especially relevant for organizations that do not have a mature metrics and reporting capability.

Step 5: Ensure that these metrics are critical to the business and part of monthly/periodic business metrics that are review by top leadership. This is why projects that are selected need to be linked to overall goals.

Step 6: During the top level metrics review, it is important to get the project champions to formally recognize the contribution to the business from the projects.

Note: In organizations that have senior executive support for the continuous improvement program, it is fine to have an exclusive dashboard for the program and a separate leadership review cadence associated with the program. However, for organizations that are just starting a continuous improvement program, it is better to include the program and project metrics within the overall corporate dashboard. This ensures right visibility to the program and projects from key stakeholders and business leaders.

Suggestion Toolbox:

It is not sufficient to just track progress on continuous improvement initiatives that have been approved or launched. If an organization truly wants to build a continuous improvement culture it needs to develop a formal process to capture and track all continuous improvement suggestions. In addition, all employees should be empowered to identify any improvement initiatives and should be given the opportunity to drive those as well, where it makes sense. A suggestion toolbox is commonly deployed by companies to solicit improvement opportunities. However, there is a change management aspect to this that should not be overlooked. If employees find out that their suggestions are not being worked on or at least looked into, they will soon lose the motivation to submit opportunities when they see one and the toolbox will get added to the long list of tools that are never used within the company.

In addition to reporting numbers and metrics and demonstrating the impact of continuous improvement initiatives, it is also extremely important to socialize the success stories with the business at large. Companies that have successful continuous improvement programs in place make use of various media internally and externally to share the stories and highlight the value the continuous improvement program brings to their business. With proper measurement and reporting mechanisms in place it also becomes very easy to provide facts and figures behind the successful initiatives and thereby give credence to the success or improvement claims.

We have been asked at times do we need a web-based dashboard or the can the dashboard reside on a desktop? The answer depends on the direction and magnitude of the program as well as the access and method of delivery of the reports. Generally speaking, for small organizations it is much easier and quicker to have a program manager of the improvement program manage the dashboard either on their own desktop or on a shared server (e.g. Microsoft SharePoint). This helps ensure that resources are not tied down maintaining the dashboard versus working on real projects. However, in the case of a cross functional deployment a web based dashboard becomes more of a necessity.

Finally, we would like to emphasize that it is very important to ensure that proper measurements are used to evaluate the success of the selected continuous improvement methodology. For example, if an organization decides to implement Total Productivity Maintenance (TPM), it is more important to measure the Overall Equipment Effectiveness as compared to a Six Sigma program that will measure percentage reduction in defect and overall cost reduction.

The table which is based on the Boston Consulting Group's Balanced Scorecard approach, shows how Six Sigma and Lean projects can be linked to core business metrics that are reviewed by senior leadership every month:

Financial Metrics:

- Increase Revenue by 5%

  o Six Sigma Project 1

  o Lean Project 1

- Reduction in Costs and Incremental Margin increase attributable to the CI Program (*Note: To the extent possible this should be tracked and reported at the executive level to demonstrate the value of the program*)

People Metrics:

- Reduce Unwanted Employee Attrition

  o Six Sigma Project 2

Customer Metrics:

- Reduce Customer Churn

  o Six Sigma Project 3

Operational Metrics:

- Increase Efficiency at Plant 1

  o Lean Project 2

- Reduce Time To Respond

  o Kaizen Event 1

Measurement Metrics and Goals for External Consultants:

What we have described above is mostly applicable for an internal program. However, a similar measurement and reporting system should be put in place even for organizations where the continuous improvement program is driven by external consultants. These metrics needs to be included in the contract between the company and the consultant(s), so that there are no ambiguities later on between the two parties. A similar reporting approach can be followed for projects driven by the external consultants.

Case Study:

A global company with a fairly large Lean Six Sigma program actually made use of a web-based dashboard to manage its continuous improvement program. The program had three Master Black Belts and ten Black Belts spread globally across multiple internal divisions in addition to one Master Black Belt who was the LSS program manager and had the overall responsibility for the dashboard. The MBBs from each division were, however, responsible for ensuring that all data related to their area of responsibility was properly represented in the dashboard. All employees could access the dashboard to see the list of active projects but did not have the authority to make any changes. This ensured the integrity and proper ownership of the data. Reports pulled from this dashboard became the "single source of truth" around the improvement program and an integral part of the company's board meetings.

Chapter 10

Final Thoughts

Good business leaders create a vision, articulate the vision, passionately own the vision, and relentlessly drive it to completion. – Jack Welch

The changing economic situation and the world order have significantly shifted how companies are approaching and running their businesses today. Most companies are facing higher competition and lower margins as their customer's spending habits have changed. At the same time we are also seeing very high unemployment rates in the United States and significant struggles with the European Union economy. Even China, which has been the fastest growing economy for last few decades, has started to see a reduction in its growth rate.

At the same time it is surprising to find many companies (and governments) are still running with processes that are wasteful and not necessarily meeting the needs of the customers (and citizens). It is our firm belief that now, more than ever, is the time to embrace structured waste reduction programs in all areas and operate more effectively and efficiently.

In this book we have tried to share our experience and knowledge that we have gained over the years both while deploying continuous improvement programs as industry leaders and as consultants, and we assume that at least this book will give business leaders a good start in identifying and deploying the proper continuous improvement program. Lean and Six Sigma have been around for years and whenever the methodologies have been properly applied, it has helped organizations achieve breakthrough improvements. It is our hope that like many business leaders who have benefitted from these methodologies, the government leaders globally will also embrace the Lean Six Sigma methodology and start reducing wastes from the governmental expenditures. That is the need of the hour.

How to Select the First Project:

And finally, we wanted to address a question that might have cropped up in the mind of the readers. How to select the *perfect* project? Well, in our opinion, it might be extremely difficult to identify a perfect project. At any given point of time an organization would have gaps in different areas, and as we discussed at several places, there are a few factors that will have to be considered in choosing the project. Summarizing the concepts we have discussed in previous chapters, assuming there is no leadership support for the continuous improvement program it will be important to find a project that can be directly linked to the corporate level goals, is a highly visible pain point for the business, has a decent chance of success, and can be completed in a relatively acceptable span of time, say three to five months. In fact, our recommendation would be to build a portfolio of projects (Six Sigma, Lean, Kaizen etc.) so that even if one project team is struggling or have figured out during the Measure or Analyze phase that the gap that was perceived at the beginning was not a gap in reality, there would be other projects that will get completed. This will give the program a decent chance to survive and thrive.

And one other thing that we would like to mention here, if you are thinking about the perfect project, you must also start thinking about the near perfect employee who can drive the project. Remember everything that we have discussed in this book is the tools that can help you get started down the path of continuous improvement. But you cannot make much progress unless you have the right resources driving the projects.

APPENDIX 1:

Assessing an Organization's Change Readiness Before Deploying a Six Sigma Program

Even though Six Sigma has been embraced globally as one of the most effective continuous improvement methodologies, we still get to hear or read occasional stories of companies that had a bad experience with their attempt to deploy Six Sigma. Probably the most notable ones that have been covered extensively and cited numerous times are the examples of 3M Corporation and Home Depot. We have briefly touched upon what we think was the problem at Home Depot from a change management perspective during the deployment of Six Sigma. In this section we will look at 3M's Six Sigma deployment failure from a change management perspective and understand what could have been done differently to get a better outcome.

In 2002, when James McNerney came to 3M Corporation from GE as their CEO, the stock price of 3M jumped by 20 percent over a period of a few days. This was because of the anticipation that McNerney was going to implement the continuous improvement program popularized by GE that by that time had become a legend in corporate circles, and it was called Six Sigma. True to the expectations McNerney announced that 3M was going to embrace the Six Sigma methodology for driving continuous improvement. However, it did not take long for the program to fail. In 2007 McNerney was replaced by George Buckley as the new CEO, and he immediately announced his intention to take a hard look at whether Six Sigma was right for the company's culture. By end of 2007, Six Sigma was dropped from the R&D division and became one of the most talked about examples used by the detractors of Six Sigma to show that the methodology does not work. So what went wrong? The common consensus is that Six Sigma is not suitable for innovative companies, that it stifles innovation, and forces people to follow a structured approach that is contrary to the inventor spirit.

However, this theory is not always true. Companies like Starwood Hotels and Resort have shown that Six Sigma can actually be used to in the innovation process to come up with new services. And if the blame for the death of 3M's legendary innovative products from 2004 to 2007 is attributed to Six Sigma, what would explain the fact that the company slipped to twenty-second place in 2008 from the seventh position in 2007, dropped altogether in 2009, and has failed to make it back into the *Bloomberg Businessweek* list of most innovative companies in 2010? So, it seems like the root cause behind the failure was not really with the Six Sigma methodology but rather the acceptance of Six Sigma. In fact, had the company done a change management assessment before deploying the program, it would have helped the leadership develop the proper deployment strategy that probably would have resulted in Six Sigma being embraced by the development community and successfully used to come up with innovative products instead of being taken as a program pushed down on them by top leadership who did not understand the company's culture.

A methodology that can help a company assess change readiness is ADKAR®. ADKAR stands for Awareness, Desire, Knowledge, Ability, and Reinforcement. It is a change management model developed by PROSCI research and is gaining tremendous acceptance in business circles as a preferred change management methodology. The reason this model works is because it shows how to identify potential barriers to change and uses a change deployment model to remove (or reduce) the impact of those barriers. The ADKAR® model is based on the basic concept that successful projects depend on three factors: leadership, project management and change management. Assuming that leadership and project management are already in place, an organization needs to focus on change management which forms the third piece of the triangle to get the expected outcome from a project or initiative.

Let us now analyze the 3M situation using the five step ADKAR® model to examine whether the deployment possibly could have been more successful.

Clearly for 3M's Six Sigma deployment there was visible and committed leadership. We can also probably assume that there was a program infrastructure put in place that would have driven the project management side as well of the deployment. However, the fact that there was significant resentment among the workforce tells us that change management piece was overlooked. The ADKAR® methodology, if carried out properly by a change management team, would have shown that the innovation team did have the awareness around the need to have a Six Sigma deployment but did not have the *desire* to stick to the Six Sigma methodology and that should have been a red flag. The leadership team moved from the *awareness* step to the *knowledge* step and had put the training and infrastructure in place to support the transformational initiative. But there was no desire on the part of the inventors and innovators to utilize this methodology. In the book *Employee's Survival Guide to Change*, Jeffrey Hiatt gives an example of a dad who was trying to make his son a better baseball player. So he purchased some coaching tapes and made his son go through them. However, even after a significant period of time there was no improvement in his son's performance. When he confronted his son, the dad realized that his son has no desire to be a better baseball player and was content with his current level of performance–he just wanted to be around with the other players and that was his motivation for playing the game. So this was a case where dad jumped from *awareness* to the *knowledge* step, whereas the effort to make his son a better player was held up because of a lack of *desire* on the son's part. This example can most likely be applied to 3M. What 3M leadership probably should have done was to show to the inventors how Six Sigma can help them in doing their job better and the "What's in it for me?" Part of the failure can also probably be attributed to the way Six Sigma was deployed more as a rigorous methodology rather than a flexible tool, and this took away the potential benefits 3M could have realized in its innovation process by selectively applying Six Sigma tools to the process.

APPENDIX 2:

Application of Continuous Improvement Across the Entire Value Chain

A medical equipment manufacturing company has identified the need for a product that can potentially revolutionize the healthcare industry. Let us look at opportunities for continuous improvement that exists over the cradle-to-grave lifecycle of the product.

As we have seen from the case study in Chapter 1, the organization pulls together a team of subject matter experts from sales and customer service organizations since they were the ones who first realized that there was a demand in the market for this revolutionary product. Representatives were also pulled in from R&D and the new product development team as well as finance and operations. The team came together for a structured brainstorming session to further pursue the concept and develop a product that would meet the need of the customers. Once the basic concept was defined, extensive customer focus groups were conducted to gather the voice of the customer. Based on the voice of the customer a House of Quality was built which is a Quality Function Deployment (QFD) tool. QFD is used extensively in Design for Six Sigma (DFSS) Projects. House of Quality incorporates customer requirements, technical requirements and a planning matrix. The planning matrix quantifies the customer requirements, compares competitors' products and assigns a weight to each of the customers' requirements. The final element of the House of Quality is a target which, among other things, gives the team a set of engineering values that need to be met by the design team.

Using the House of Quality approach the team was able to come up with alternative product concepts that could potentially satisfy the customers' needs. The team then used a Pugh matrix to compare the different potential product concepts against each other and identify whether a particular product which is called the datum is better, same or worse than the alternative products based on various factors (Note: the datum can be any one randomly chosen from the list of different solutions)-in this particular case the team used time to market, ROI, Designed for Manufacturability, Designed for Supply Chain etc. as some of the factors. The finally selected product concept was then handed over to the R&D team to design the product.

At the same time that the concept was being finalized, the project deliverables and performance measures were entered in the annual Hoshin Kanri plan so that they could be measured and tracked during the periodic Hoshin reviews. This gave the message to all the team members that executive leadership was supportive of this project. A Change Management Plan was put together as well, and the change manager used the ADKAR® model to deploy the Change Management Plan.

The new product launch team also got engaged to ensure the right vendors were selected who had Lean manufacturing capability and could manufacture the new product. A Kaizen event was held at the finally selected manufacturer's plant and a detailed failure mode and effects analysis was conducted to determine potential defects that could get introduced during the design as well as manufacturing, stocking, and shipping processes and what should be done to eliminate or minimize the impact of the failure modes.

The company traditionally had a higher time to implement solutions and equipment at customer locations compared to the best in class competitors. A Six Sigma team was put together to understand the root causes behind the high time to implement with a goal of reducing it by 50 percent. The new product team was roped into the Six Sigma project as subject matter experts to ensure that the new product could be implemented in an extremely short time frame from when the customer contract was signed.

Even though the initial market response was euphoric and customer demand was extremely high for the revolutionary product, the team found a few issues. First, since the product was new, there were frequent shutdowns of the equipment, and it needed service support and the customers called in frequently to the service desk to get technical assistance and troubleshooting help. However, the time to restore customer issues was taking way longer than what was contractually committed to leading to missed service level agreement credits as well as dissatisfied customers. Second, the product required parts to be stored in the field and the field service engineers were complaining about the field parts quality. And finally, the dead on arrival (DOA) rate for the product was higher than initially estimated leading to decreased profit margins and customer dissatisfaction. This was also true for the units that were repaired and sold in the secondary market or as backup units usually kept by the customers at their locations.

For the first problem, a Six Sigma team was formed that followed the DMAIC methodology to get to the root cause behind the delay in restoration of customer outages. Once the root causes were uncovered, for example there was no easy way for a service desk agent to determine what the problem was that the customer was facing, lack of training, improper staffing etc., the team developed solutions to address the issues and improved the time to restore by more than 60 percent.

Reverse logistics: Another root cause behind the DOA was found to be the repair process. This was determined through a three-day Gemba Kaizen event that was conducted at the repair vendors and the team observed the entire process from the time the product entered the repair shop to the time it was shipped out. Gemba Kaizen approach focuses on the workplace versus conventional Kaizen events that can be conducted at remote locations.

APPENDIX 3:

Other Commonly Adopted Continuous Improvement Methodologies

Even though this book focuses extensively on Six Sigma and Lean methodologies, any business leader who is considering the deployment of a CI program should not get into the mindset of choosing either or both of the two. They should be looked at purely as tools within the overall process improvement methodology and remember to focus on change management around people who will be asked to embrace a process improvement methodology. The basic concept of any continuous improvement initiative is based on the Shewhart or Deming philosophy of the PDCA cycle. What Six Sigma or Lean does is to put the proper structure and approach around this methodology and train the practitioners to be able to pick the right tools and apply them, as needed, to reach the end goal of increased quality and reduced costs as evangelized by Deming. Also follow the advice of Joseph M. Juran and Peter Senge to make quality an integral part of the overall corporate level business plan. Note that reduced costs include soft costs like customer and employee satisfaction or productivity gain that allow an employee to focus on his or her own career development. This is not necessarily a hard savings though, but it is still contributing to the overall success of the corporation.

We have already covered the concepts of Six Sigma, Lean, and Kaizen in previous chapters. Now let us look at some of the other commonly applied continuous improvement methodologies.

TRIZ Methodology:

TRIZ is a creative problem solving methodology. It is a Russian acronym for "Theory of Inventive Problem Solving" and G.S. Altshuller and his colleagues are credited with the development of this methodology. This methodology has been around in what was then called the USSR from around the 1950s and has gained significant popularity globally in the last decade or so. It is being used both as a tool for Six Sigma process improvement initiatives as well as a standalone tool. The fundamental premise of this methodology is that someone somewhere has experienced a problem that is similar to what you are facing, and if you can find that problem and the solution, you can solve the current problem as well, though it might be in a totally different setting or context. The methodology works by linking the current problem to a similar TRIZ problem (which can be searched from TRIZ databases), understanding what the solution to that TRIZ problem was, and using creative brainstorming to develop a solution to the current problem. In fact, there is a list of Forty Principles of Problem Solving that were identified by the researchers who developed the methodology through sixty-five years of research and these forty were found to repeat across different fields and can be used to find solution to several common problems.

Below is an example of one principle and how it can be used to come up with creative solutions. This was published in www.triz-journal.com in 1997.

Principle 1: Segmentation

> A. *Divide an object into independent parts.*
>   o *Replace mainframe computer with personal computers.*
>   o *Replace a large truck with a truck and trailer.*
>   o *Use a work breakdown structure for a large project.*

B. *Make an object easy to disassemble.*
- o *Modular furniture*
- o *Quick disconnect joints in plumbing*

C. *Increase the degree of fragmentation or segmentation.*
- o *Replace solid shades with Venetian blinds.*
- o *Use powdered welding metal instead of foil or rod to get better penetration of the joint.*

Business Process Management:

Business Process Management is a process improvement methodology that focuses on aligning the processes of a company with the requirements of the customer. Note that Business Process *Management* is different from Business Process *Measurement*. Business Process Management takes a holistic approach to managing all aspects of an organization and aligning with the needs of the client. So in a sense Business Process Management starts with understanding the critical to customer needs and then mapping the value chain that provides the good or service that meets the customer's needs. Business Process Management focuses on current situation assessment and ultimately capturing the current processes and identifying opportunities to improve the process. Usually Business Process Management is done in today's world using process automation software and this dependence on technology differentiates Business Process Management from other continuous improvement methodologies. The Business Process Management lifecycle has six components:

Vision – business functions are designed around the strategic goals and vision of an organization. Each functional head is responsible for a certain set of processes aligned with the business vision.

Design – capturing the as-is and to-be process flow along with information flow, participants, outputs, critical to quality, etc.

Modeling – once the processes are captured, modeling helps in "what-if" analysis.

Execution – done through automation or a combination of automation and human interaction.

Monitoring – track statistics on performance of one or multiple processes and improve connected processes.

Optimization – based on process performance information the business determines areas for improvement.

Total Productivity Maintenance (TPM):

The basic philosophy of Total Productivity Maintenance is to improve productivity by making machines (and processes) more reliable and less wasteful. Total Productivity Maintenance originated in Japan in the early 1970s in the manufacturing industry, but most of the concepts can be equally applied to the transactional or service industry. TPM focuses on training and empowering the operator or service personnel to maintain the process, so that it does not deteriorate and is always capable of meeting the process requirements. It is generally used as a concept in support of Lean Manufacturing. Like Lean, TPM focuses on the seven types of waste and then works systematically to eliminate them. Since TPM is generally applied to an entire organization's process (or manufacturing line), senior level training, buy in, and sponsorship become extremely critical for successful deployment. Autonomous Maintenance, Focused Improvement, Planned Maintenance, Training and Education, Early Equipment Management (which includes Equipment Design), Quality Maintenance (understanding process capability), Office TPM and Safety & Environment are considered as the eight standard pillars on TPM. In addition, some FMCG companies like Unilever and P&G have included Supply Chain Management as the ninth TPM focus area.

Statistical Process Control:

As the name suggests, Statistical Process Control (SPC) extensively uses control charts to understand and keep track of how the critical processes are doing and takes corrective action if the process goes outside the control or specification limits.

The basic SPC process was developed by Walter Shewhart, and he is occasionally called the father of statistical process control. The limitation with Statistical Process Control is that these are rarely successful as companywide initiatives. SPC programs are more successful in a manufacturing process and work on the concept of control charts and control limits that help identify special cause and normal cause variations in a process. SPC also has some usage in the service industry, but the biggest shortfall of this approach is that it does not facilitate understanding of the softer side of a process that can impact the output of the process, like human interactions, behavior, etc. and any need for change management. However, SPC can be a very powerful tool when surgically applied to the right process to drive improvements that meet the overall business goal.

Usually a proven CI practitioner who has been exposed to the Lean or Six Sigma tools can help drive any CI program irrespective of the methodology chosen.

APPENDIX 4:

Why Continuous Improvement Specialists Fail?

We have covered the reasons why continuous improvement programs fail in Chapter 8. One of the reasons we mentioned is that having the right people in CI roles is very critical. Here we are discussing why the continuous improvement professionals fail assuming all the other factors we have mentioned for a successful program are in place. More often than not this is one of the biggest reasons why CI programs fail. We believe these are the differentiating factors between the people who thrive in the continuous improvement roles and those who struggle:

1. Stop learning: We often see the CI professionals stop learning after they have achieved certification. They are content with what they know and don't show the urge to continue to increase their learning and knowledge. However, the successful CI professional believes in continuous learning, and they are open to learning new tactics and approaches all the time. There is a belief in the continuous improvement world that continuous improvement really means "continuous learning" and those who stop learning will not have a good outing in the continuous improvement field.

2. Not open to outside ideas/opinions: Sometimes CI people are too focused in their own activities and closed for listening to outside ideas and opinions. The successful specialists are always listening and openly solicit others' views and

opinions. They are in a constant hunt to find best practices within and outside their organizations and applying them.

3.   Too long in their roles: When someone is in the same role for a long time, they become too close to the process and are unable to find further improvements. Often what we have observed with struggling CI people is that they spent more time on non-value added activities than value added activities. On the other hand, successful CI people constantly analyze their own activities and identify ways to improve their own work.

4.   Does not have the leadership discipline required: If there is one function that truly tests your leadership skills, it is the continuous improvement roles. You have to walk the talk and lead by example, not just the talk and preaching. A simple example would be if you are training everyone on the 5S of Lean and ask them to implement and maintain 5S in their areas, you better keep your own office complaint with 5S and be an example for it. If you do not keep your office 5S complaint, you are telling everyone 5S is not that important.

REFERENCES:

Chapter 1:

1. http://en.wikipedia.org/wiki/Lean_manufacturing

2. Spencer E. Ante, Six Sigma Kick Starts Starwood, Businessweek August 30, 2007 (http://www.businessweek.com/innovate/content/aug 2007/id20070830_103596.htm)

3. Kirsten Terry, Randy Woods, "Best Places to Work for Six Sigma Professionals"; iSixSigma Magazine, March/April 2011

4. Bell, Orzen; Lean IT–Enabling and Sustaining your Lean Transformation, CRC Press 2011

5. Fran Golden, MSC Opera passengers tell of mutiny during power loss, The Cruise Log, USA Today, May 11, 2011

6. Yoji Akao, Hoshin Kanri–Policy Deployment for Successful TQM, Productivity Press, 1991

7. Henderson, Larco, "Lean Transformation – How to Change your Business into a Lean Enterprise", The Oaklea Press, November 2003

8. Michael Porter, "What is Strategy", Harvard Business Review, November-December 1996

9. Gary Hamel, "Why Companies Fail – Part I", WSJ Blogs, June 1, 2009

10. Gary Hamel, "Why Companies Fail – Part II", WSJ Blogs, June 8, 2009

11. Pete Babich, "Hoshin Handbook" 3rd Edition, Total Quality Engineering, Inc., June 2007

Chapter 2:

1- John S. Ramberg, "Six Sigma: Fad or Fundamental", Quality Digest - http://www.qualitydigest.com/may00/html/sixsigmapro.html

2- JD Sicilia, Director, "Department of Defense Lean Six Sigma Deployment", Department of Defense and Department of Defense Lean Program Office, 23rd September 2008 (Unclassified)

3- Strong America Now, www.strongamericanow.org

4- Strong America Now founder pushes waste reduction as deficit solution, 14th June 2011, http://thegazette.com/2011/06/14/strong-america-now-founder-pushes-waste-reduction-as-deficit-solution/

Chapter 3:

1. Kirsten Terry, Randy Woods, "Best Places to Work for Six Sigma Professionals"; iSixSigma Magazine, March/April 2011

2. Dave Nave, "How to Compare Six Sigma, Lean and The Theory of Constraints"; Quality Progress, March 2002

3. Pande, Neuman, Cavanagh; "The Six Sigma Way", McGraw-Hill 2000

4. Jack Welch with John A. Byrne, "Jack Straight From The Gut", Warner Business Books, 2001

Chapter 4:

1. Wikipedia – CMMI -
   http://en.wikipedia.org/wiki/Capability_Maturity_Mo
   del_Integration

2. Digital Elite Top 100 IT companies
   http://images.businessweek.com/ss/10/05/0520_it_10
   0/5.htm

3. ITIL V3 Foundation Handbook – Pocketbook from
   the Official Publisher of ITIL

4. http://www.sei.cmu.edu/reports/05tn005.pdf

5. Green Six Sigma:
   http://www.mfrtech.com/articles/2034.html

6. http://smart-
   grid.tmcnet.com/news/2011/06/02/5549653.htm
   Gartner Supply Chain rankings 2011

7. ITIL Continual Service Improvement – Office of
   Government Commerce, TSO, 2007

8. Project Management Institute, A Guide To The
   Project Management Body of Knowledge – Fourth
   Edition, ANSI/PMI 99-001-2008

Chapter 5:

1. Chris F. Jones, Evaluate your Consultant's
   Performance; Summit: Canada's Magazine on Public
   Sector Purchasing, June 2009

Chapter 6:

1. Kirsten Terry, Randy Woods, "Best Places to Work
   for Six Sigma Professionals"; iSixSigma Magazine,
   March/April 2011

Chapter 7:

1. Human Change Management – Herding Cats, PwC

2. Jeffrey M. Hiatt, ADKAR – A Model for Change in Business, Government and our Community, Prosci Research 2006

3. William Bridges – Managing Transitions, Making the Most of Change, Da Capo Press, May 2003

4. Dave Bhattacharya – Driving Six Sigma Successes Without Top Level Support, iSixSigma.com, June 2011

5. Christopher Del Angel and Christina Pritchard, "What Went Wrong with Six Sigma?", Cygnus Supply & Demand Chain Executive, January 12th, 2011 – Change Management

6. Managing the change to a Lean organization http://ezinearticles.com/?Managing-the-Change-to-a-Lean-Organization&id=2450554

7. "Out at Home Depot – Behind the Flameout of Controversial CEO Bob Nardelli", Bloomberg Businessweek, January 15, 2007

8. Best Practices in Change Management – Prosci Benchmarking Report

9. Christopher Del Angel and Joe Froelich, "Six Sigma: What Went Wrong?"; destinationCRM.com, November 2008

10. At 3M, A Struggle Between Efficiency And Creativity, Bloomberg Businessweek, June11 2007

Chapter 8:

1. Christopher Del Angel and Christina Pritchard, "What Went Wrong With Six Sigma?", Cygnus

Supply & Demand Chain Executive, January 12th, 2011 – Change Management

2. Teresa Amabile and Mukti Khaire, "Creativity and the Role of the Leader," Harvard Business Review (October 2008)

3. Hecke, Callahan, Kolar, Paller, "The Brain Advantage" Becoming a More Effective Business Leader using the latest Brain Research, Prometheus Books, 2010

4. Jon Hansen, 'The Key Principles Behind The Integrated Enterprise Excellence Methodology White Paper', Ottawa, Canada 2009

5. http://www.designnews.com/article/12089-3M_Shelves_Six_Sigma_in_R_D.php

6. http://www.businessweek.com/magazine/content/07_24/b4038406.htm

7. http://www.thefabricator.com/article/shopstrategies/lean-implementation-failures LEAN FAILURE

8. http://ezinearticles.com/?6-Reasons-Why-Lean-Manufacturing-and-Six-Sigma-Fails&id=770916

9. Fayazuddin A Shirazi, "Is Six Sigma a Hard Sell Now?", Chief Executive.net, November 13, 2007

10. Dave Bhattacharya – Driving Six Sigma Successes Without Top Level Support, iSixSigma.com, June 2011

Chapter 9:

1. JD Sicilia, Department of Defense Lean Six Sigma Deployment, Department of Defense Lean Six Sigma Program Office, 23rd Sept 2008 (Source: http://www.asq509.org/ht/a/GetDocumentAction/i/32692)

Appendix 1:

1. At 3M, A Struggle Between Efficiency And Creativity, Bloomberg Businessweek, June11 2007

2. Jeffrey M. Hiatt, ADKAR A Model for Change in Business, Government and Our Community, How to Implement Successful Change in Our Personal Lives and Professional Careers, Prosci Research

3. Jeffrey Hiatt, Employees Survival Guide to Change, PROSCI publication

Appendix 3:

1. 40 Inventive Principles with Examples: http://www.triz-journal.com/archives/1997/07/b/index.html

2. Malcolm Jones, "Lean, Six Sigma or TPM"; Manufacturing Today, November, December 2006

About the Authors

Dave Bhattacharya is the lead author and has sixteen years of experience in multiple industries and countries. With niche specialties as diverse as design engineering, materials management, strategic sourcing, supply chain management, continuous improvement, project management, change management, as well as IT strategy and service delivery, he is currently a management consultant with Slalom Consulting. In the past, he has led and deployed Lean Six Sigma Program in a multi-billion dollar global organization and has been the Director of Continuous Improvement in a global IT services organization. In addition to being a certified Six Sigma Master Black Belt and Lean Kaizen expert, he is certified in ISO9000, Prosci Change Management, and ITIL v3 as well as in production and inventory management by the Association of Operations Management. He is also an expert in Hoshin Kanri deployment. He holds a bachelor's in mechanical engineering from University of Calcutta and an MBA in finance and supply chain management from Michigan State University.

Jayaprakash Gnanam is the co-author and founder and CEO of Lean Six Sigma Experts Corporation, training and consulting organization based in the US with offices in India and the UK. He has significant experience in implementing and training Lean Six Sigma in the US, India, Europe, and South America. He has held almost all Lean Six Sigma roles in various multinational companies over the last decade ranging from Lean intern to global director of Lean Six Sigma. He has trained and mentored several professionals in Lean Six Sigma around the world. He has a master's in industrial and systems engineering from Colorado State University-Pueblo. He is a certified Lean Six Sigma Master Black Belt, Lean Trainer/Practitioner, ASQ Black Belt, ASQ Quality Engineer, and ASQ Manager of Quality and Organizational Excellence.

LSSE Publication
www.leansixsigmaexperts.com

Good Luck with your CI Journey!

Thanks!

JP hnanam